BROTHER VAN

MONTANA PIONEER CIRCUIT RIDER

• • •

D1603203

BROTHER VAN

MONTANA PIONEER
CIRCUIT RIDER

Robert W. Lind, Ph.D.

• • •

Library of Congress Catalog Card Number: 92-71600
ISBN: 1-56044-145-3

Published by Robert W. Lind, Ph.D., 3771 East Crellin Circle, Las Vegas, Nevada 89120, in cooperation with SkyHouse Publishers, an imprint of Falcon Press Publishing Co., Inc., Helena, Montana.

Design, typesetting, and other prepress work by Falcon Graphics, Helena, Montana.

Distributed by Falcon Press Publishing Co., Inc., P.O. Box 1718, Helena, Montana 59624, or call 1-800-582-2665.

First Edition

Manufactured in the United States of America.

In Gratitude For Having The One Great Gift
That Was Denied To Brother Van,
This Book Is Dedicated To
My Wife And Children

• • •

William Wesley Van Orsdel 1848-1919
The legendary Montana Methodist minister

Foreword

• • •

*H*e was a living legend in his own time. And when he died in 1919, the words that were written about him by Bishop Cooke had been accepted as truth for years everywhere in Montana:

> I don't believe there was a dog in Montana that would not wag his tail when he saw him coming.

For forty-seven years the pioneer people of the new state had seen him coming. First across the prairie and mountain trails afoot or on horseback, and later by road and railroad, William Wesley Van Orsdel traveled Montana's vast domain. And as he traveled the long name had been shortened to "Brother Van," and the short man's shadow had lengthened to touch the lives and institutions of the Territory and State.

Brother Van and Montana were ideally suited to each other. Van had the calling in his heart to "go west and build on no other man's foundations." Montana, in 1872, was being settled by rugged pioneer folk who had left other men's foundations behind them in the east. The long trek west has sorted out those who could not endure the hardships of new beginnings. As the pioneer saying went, "The cowards never started and the weaklings fell by the wayside."

To paint a word picture of the pioneer preacher and the pioneer territory which captures the real feeling Brother Van had for Montana and which Montana had for Brother Van is almost impossible. But Bob Lind, a part of the church which

Brother Van helped to establish, has come closer than any writer to date.

Lind's picture of Brother Van and his times is reliably accurate, though it was no easy task to detach fact from fiction in giving account of a man about whom stories grew like grass on the Montana prairie. He found in Brother Van's life so much adventure and color that he only needed to tell the story as it was.

When you finish reading this book you will have met the best of the early frontier in the Rocky Mountain West. You will follow a man who made a pulpit for preaching the Good News out of the freighter's or cowboy's camp, the cabin or the ranch home, the Indian tepee, the barroom or the street corner. And you will see that to all of his congregations, formal or informal, he always gave his best in word and song.

He saw the watering places of the buffalo and the antelope become the campground of the cowboy and sheepherder. These oftentimes gave way to the ranches and towns. He saw the wide places in the trails become cities. He saw the wildlife give way to domesticated animals; he saw the great prairies turn into golden wheat fields. "To meet these challenges there were no trails, but Brother Van made them and showed us how to follow them," a Montana Methodist spokesman said of him.

The frontiers have changed somewhat now, though thousands of square miles of wilderness area still remain in Montana. Life's hard problems still remain, too, and those who would conquer them must be the spiritual descendants of Brother Van—pioneers of the way which is always waiting to make people and situations new.

The Reverend George A. Harper
Retired Minister of the
Yellowstone Conference of the
United Methodist Church
Helena, Montana

Brother Van

By Mrs. Margaret Carlyle McIlveen
Written in 1912 as part of the festivities held at
Fort Benton in honor of the fortieth anniversary
of Brother Van's arrival in Montana on July 1, 1872.

What, stranger, do I hear aright?
You say, "Who is this man?"
Well, you must be a tenderfoot
To not know Brother Van!

In North Montana Conference
He is a D. S. now;
And that important post, none
Could better fill, I'll vow.

Yes sir, there's an honest heart.
Each man he claims as brother;
His life's a sermon on the text,
"Love ye one another."

He's one of our sturdy pioneers,
Of noble Daniel's band,
Who bravely stood for truth and God
In fair Montana's land.

In hardships oft, yet undismayed,
He dared to stand alone;
Like Jacob in the wilderness,
His pillow oft a stone.

This consecrated man went forth
O'er mountain, vale and glen,
And preached to all of peace on earth
And God's goodwill toward men.

And foremost still with genial smile
And love toward every man;
And ever-ready sympathy,
Is our good brother, Van.

Yes sir, a blessing he has been
Since forty years ago
In Gettysburg he left his home
And came with heart aglow.

In fair Montana's land he longed
'Gainst sin and wrong to fight;
He came with consecrated heart,
He came with pockets light.

A journey long, Iowa reached,
He sought to work his way;
"Half fare," the Captain cried, "if you
Will sing and preach and pray."

And well they sped and well the youth
Repaid the Captain's care;
Whose eyes were moist with grateful tears
As he returned the fare.

'Twas at Fort Benton, July first
Eighteen seventy-two,
That young Van Orsdel stepped ashore,
His Master's work to do.

He lost no time; that very day
Fort Benton there beheld
The first Protestant services
In north Montana held.

Van Orsdel had the gift of song.
He used it in God's way;
His singing filled the halls with men
Who won't forget that day.

He traveled east, he traveled west,
And, welcomed everywhere,
He told the gospel message sweet
In sermon, song and prayer.

If sickness, sorrow, pain or grief
On anyone should fall,
Then Brother Van with sympathy
Responded to their call.

Through many a scene of wild-west life
Of forty years ago,
Through dangers, oft, of storm and flood,
This man of God did go.

And when against Nez Perces they
Formed a protective plan,
Thirty volunteers rode forth,
And one was Brother Van.

His mind is broad, the mind of Christ,
Who would the world embrace;
No prejudice hath he 'gainst men
Because of creed or race.

And thus for more than forty years
This minister of God
Hath in our midst, with blameless life,
His pilgrim pathway trod.

His hearty handclasp, cheerful voice,
His faith in God and man
Makes friends of all, so he became
The People's Brother Van.

Introduction

• • •

The biography of Brother Van
recounts the life of a frontier circuit rider of legendary
proportions who sang, preached and prayed his way into
the hearts of the people and the history of Montana. It is a
love story, a story of Indians on the warpath, and a story of
life on the western frontier. But most of all, it is a story of
the indomitable, never-say-die faith of a man whose
charismatic power drew to him people from every walk of
life, from governors to gunslingers.

Brother Van was a warmly human character who became
the most known and best-loved man in Montana. He
happened also to be a Methodist preacher who founded
more than a hundred churches, a university, half a dozen
hospitals and a children's home in his 47-year ministry,
from 1872 to 1919, besides overseeing the building of at
least 50 Methodist parsonages. The account of his life is
compelling, inspiring and often exciting.

He was a simple man, but he was not inconsequential. He
was, without question, the man of the hour in his time, and
would have been a giant figure on the scene wherever and
whenever he had lived. He happened to live in Montana
during its critical formative years, and he exerted a significant influence upon events in Montana's history.

The Blackfeet Indians who gave him the honorary tribal
membership and the chieftain's title of "Great-Heart" had
captured his essence. His heart was great; he was able to
embrace in Christian love persons from every walk of life,

and could relate to them—no matter where he found them—in saloons as readily as in church.

This is a story about the power of personal commitment. Almost anyone could have done what Brother Van did, if he had the same marvelous singing voice, the same warmth and depth of spirit, the same zeal for souls, and the same Dutch-stubborn faith that would not bend or break no matter how severely tested. Brother Van always looked forward confidently to victory no matter how bleak the present prospects may have been. It is a story about what can happen when God gets to make use of all a person's powers and gifts, with absolutely nothing held back.

Brother Van was fortunate to have come to Montana at a time when he was able to hold the first preaching service, perform the first baptism or wedding, or hold the first communion service or Christian burial in a large number of places. To be there first and do things that haven't been done before is a privilege not given to many, but he was such a unique and charismatic person that he would have been extraordinary wherever and whenever he had lived.

Anatole France said, "Historical books which contain no lies are extremely tedious." I hope and believe he was wrong. Truth may not only be stranger than fiction, but more interesting, since we have the assurance these things really happened. This book contains no known or deliberate fabrications. It was carefully researched over a very long period of time, and all of the material in the book concerning Brother Van's life and work is supported by his own handwritten journals, by letters that were written by him or to him, and by first-hand written or verbal accounts of people who had known him.

Quotations from Brother Van's journals and from letters written by him and to him are presented exactly as written, the author having successfully resisted the strong temptation to correct the sometimes unique spelling and punctuation of the original documents.

The author is appreciative of the assistance rendered by his long-time friend, George Harper, and by Rick Newby of Falcon Press in Helena, and for the cooperation given by the United Methodist Historical Society of the Yellowstone Annual Conference and the staff of the Paul M. Adams Library at Rocky Mountain College.

This book represents, as readers will readily note, a total revision and rewriting of the book "From the Ground Up" that was published in 1961. The basic facts of Brother Van's life and work have not changed in the past 30 years, of course, so the same story as before is retold in a different way in this edition. I hope that you will be pleased with what I have done.

Robert W. Lind, Ph.D.
Retired Minister of the
Montana Conference of the
United Methodist Church
Las Vegas, Nevada
February 6, 1992

Chapter One

• • •

Will knew the crowd of people on the levee was not a welcoming party in his honor. There wasn't a soul in all the region who knew he was coming, or who he was, for that matter. But the arrival of a riverboat at Fort Benton, Montana Territory, meant that the frontiersmen would receive some fairly recent news of events in far-off places such as Sioux City, St. Louis, Chicago and cities even further east. It was a social event of some significance to nearly everyone on the frontier.

Although it was only seven o'clock on a Sunday morning, people of just about every description were on hand as the *Far West* tied up at the levee. Strings of freight wagons, drawn by long teams of oxen, were on hand to receive the ship's cargo and deliver it to local businesses and residents. Soldiers from the nearby fort that gave the place its name were there to receive the cargo designated for the army. Other wagons were there to collect the freight that would go overland to Sun River, Fort Shaw, Helena and other places beyond the head of navigation. Many of those who had gathered at the levee had no particular business to conduct, but were interested onlookers.

The railroad lines that were connecting many cities in the East and Midwest would not relieve the remoteness of the

West for another decade or more. The best way to go West was to travel by riverboat as far as was possible, and then go by horse-drawn coach or on horseback, or walk, if one's destination was further inland. Not many miles upstream from Fort Benton were the great falls of the Missouri River. Not truly a waterfall, in actuality it was an incredible series of downward-stepping shelves of rock. In the space of around 10 miles, these steps dropped the level of the river some 400 feet. The presence of the great falls made Fort Benton the head of navigation on the Missouri, and thus it became one of the most prominent places in the history of the westward expansion.

Fort Benton began in 1831 as a center for fur trading, making it the oldest settlement in the mountain west. "Its true historic career embraced only around half a century, but in those few years, it saw more romance, tragedy and vigorous life than many a city a hundred times its size and ten times its age," wrote Hiram Chittenden in 1903.

Alexander Culbertson, working out of Fort McKenzie some 200 miles to the east, developed fur trading with the Blackfeet Indians, who had been a sullen and warlike tribe when he first encountered them. The Blackfeet had been swindled in earlier years by some unscrupulous traders, and it took the work of Culbertson and others to win their confidence again. It was his successful trading that created the need for a shipping point near the head of navigation. The first name given it was Fort Lewis. Fort Lewis was built on the Teton River, a tributary of the Marias River, which is a tributary of the Missouri River, all of which converge near Fort Benton. Later, the fort was moved to the Fort Benton location, but was still called Fort Lewis for several years. The fort was rebuilt in adobe style, and on Christmas night 1850, it was formally reopened under the name of Fort Benton, so named in honor of Senator Thomas H. Benton (U. S. Senator from Missouri), who was a frequent champion and defender of the West's fur trade.

The first steamboat arrived at Fort Benton in 1859, and the official townsite was laid out in 1865. The young city grew rapidly, along with the riverboat commerce. It was reported that on June 11th, 1866, there were seven steamboats tied up at the Fort Benton landing.

Although it was originally established to serve the fur trade forty years earlier, Fort Benton's importance now had very little to do with furs. Its current role had to do with the settling of the West, and young Will Van Orsdel had become a part of that influx. While some vessels that plied the river carried several hundred passengers, Will was the lone passenger on the *Far West*. The forts and other settlements along the river, as well as the towns that were springing up further inland, created an enormous demand for goods from the East. Many boats operated with great profit to their owners by carrying cargo, and had very little cabin space other than that which was needed to house the ship's crew. The *Far West* was such a cargo ship, capable of carrying a payload of 400 tons.

She was practically a new vessel, 190 feet long and 33 feet wide, having been built in Pittsburgh, Pennsylvania, just two years before, in 1870. During the earlier years of riverboat commerce, most vessels had been "sidewheelers." The *Far West* was a "sternwheeler," burly enough to carry a substantial payload, and yet light enough to be speedy and maneuverable. She was able to navigate in as little as 20 inches of water, whereas the older sidewheelers usually needed well over twice that for safe travel. With a full 400-ton load, the ship drew 54 inches of water as she plowed through the water propelled by her twin 15 inch diameter steam engines. Workmen labored constantly to feed wood into her three boilers. Going upstream with a good load of cargo, such a boat would consume 6 to 8 cords of wood per day. Considering all the boats that had plied the river for a number of years, it was already becoming obvious that the availability of wood was going to be the limiting factor in the expansion of riverboat commerce. Every day the *Far West* burned a pile of wood equal to the full width of the ship, 33 feet, cut into 4 foot lengths, and stacked 7 feet high—7-8 cords. The older and larger sidewheelers burned 10 to 12 cords of wood per day.

The gentle rain that was falling did nothing to dampen Will's enthusiasm for the moment he had so long awaited. As protection against the rain and chill of the early, cloudy morning, Will had donned a black coat which partially obscured the fact that his stocky Dutch frame was covered by his best, and only, black suit. The longer fringes of his blond hair stuck out under the headband of his wide-brimmed black hat. His blue eyes fairly danced with the excitement he felt finally to be where he knew the Lord had called him. Somehow he knew that this day—Sunday, July first, 1872—was the day his life would most truly began.

Anxious as he was to be on his way, it seemed to Will as though the crew would never get the gangplank in place so that he could debark, although they gave the appearance of working with their usual skill and efficiency. But nothing in his twenty-four years had prepared him for what he encountered when he had reached the end of the gangplank. By the time he had taken three steps, Will's feet were so heavy with the sticky clay that he could scarcely lift them. Later he learned that to Montanans this was "gumbo." In vast areas of the state, both east and west, the fertile soil, when wet, turns to a sticky clay that adheres to anything it touches. He noted that he seemed to get taller every step he took, as the size of the gumbo clumps under his feet increased.

Putting one foot in front of the other became a major

accomplishment for Will, but most of those standing on the levee were polite enough not to display too much enjoyment in the struggles of this nice-looking young greenhorn. It was a lesson they had all learned once: when it rains in Montana, walking outdoors is a real challenge. It's best not to step anywhere on wet earth if you can avoid it.

As soon as he had made it to the gathering of people, Will singled out a rather distinguished-looking man and introduced himself. "Good morning, sir, I'm William Wesley Van Orsdel, a Methodist preacher, and I'm wondering if there is a place in town where I could hold services, this being the Sabbath." There was a collective gasp from those standing near enough to hear. Preachers were a rarity indeed in Fort Benton, and those who had been seen were Roman Catholic. So far as anyone could recall, there had never been a Protestant preacher who held services in Fort Benton.

Will had made a fortunate choice, for the man he had spoken to replied in a friendly manner, "I'm very happy to meet you, parson. My name is Tattan, Judge Tattan. The courthouse where I hold forth is just down the street a little ways, and it's not in use Sundays. Don't see any reason why you couldn't hold church there, if you'd like." Will lost no time accepting the offer. He couldn't believe his luck, being offered a place to have church services upon his very first inquiry.

Making his way down the street toward the building the judge had indicated as the court house, Will paused every couple of steps to try to shake off some of the gumbo which clung so tenaciously to his boots. He soon learned that the problem was somewhat self-limiting, for once his shoes had attracted just so much of the sticky stuff, with each new step he lost about the same amount as he acquired. The boot scrapers that were mounted outside the doors of many buildings, or a strong sharp stick, were about the only means

*Brother Van (age 28) as he looked when
he came to Montana.*

of getting enough of it off that one would feel all right about stepping indoors.

Reaching the court house was the longest block's walk Will had ever taken, and as soon as he arrived at the small adobe structure and looked inside, he knew Judge Tattan had never happened to hold court on a rainy day. It was raining almost as hard inside the building as it was outside. The difference was that the rain outdoors came down clear and clean, while that which fell indoors was muddied by its passage through the dirt roof. Indoors, the footing was no less muddy and sticky than it had been on the street he had just traversed. It didn't take Will long to decide that there must be a better place than this to launch his ministry in Montana.

Studying the main street from the court house doorway, Will noticed that not too many doors down the street was one of the town's major businesses, with a substantial front entrance that had a roof and a wooden plank floor. The sign over the entrance said "BAKER'S GENERAL STORE," and it appeared to be open on this early Sunday morning. Will made it to the store with little difficulty and found Mr. Baker himself inside behind the counter. Baker was no less pleased and surprised than Judge Tattan had been to learn that the newcomer was a Methodist preacher, and he, like most of the others, would be happy to attend a church service. Most of those on the frontier had not been to a regular church service since they had left their homes in the East; going to church would be a little bit like going home. It would be a point of contact with a civilized world they had long since left behind.

After an exchange of greetings, Mr. Baker told Will, "There's a Roman Catholic priest in town right now, named Father Van Gorp. He's holding services just a couple doors down the street in a vacant store building owned by T. C. Powers, and I'm sure it would be just fine for you to use it, too. In fact, I expect I'll be seeing him soon, and I'll speak to him about it."

Following Baker's directions, Will went to the Powers building and stepped inside, finding the priest preparing for his morning mass. "Father Van Gorp, I'm Will Van Orsdel, a Methodist preacher," Will said, offering his hand. Van Gorp was as delighted as he was astonished to find a fellow clergyman in this remote outpost. The priest told Will that he had been working for some time in the various prairie settlements further inland, and that after his services today, he was taking the first riverboat downstream on which he could find passage, and would hope for a more peaceful tour of duty in a more settled place, such as St.Louis. An obvious bond of brotherhood existed between them, despite the fact that they were Methodist and Roman Catholic, and there was serious distrust and lack of understanding between the two denominations in the states far to the east. The frontier exerted a great levelling influence upon all kinds of people, Will would learn. It created a sort of classless society, in a way. People were accepted at face value, not for pretensions and airs.

Will explained to Father Van Gorp his mission of the moment, that of finding a place for holding Sunday worship services, and the priest quickly suggested just as the storekeeper Baker had done, "Why don't you use this place? I'll be done with my service before long. I've found Mr. Powers to be a kind and generous man, and I'm certain he'd be pleased to have you make use of it." It wasn't a cathedral by any stretch of the imagination, but it afforded excellent protection from the rain and the gumbo. Compared to the adobe court house, it could almost seem to be a cathedral. It seemed quite ideal to Will, and he told his Roman Catholic friend, "I'll be happy to hold my service here, and, if you don't mind, I'd like very much to stay here and attend your service."

"I'd be very pleased if you would," Van Gorp replied, as he turned to make the final preparations for the beginning of his service.

As he listened to Father Van Gorp preach on the text "What does it profit a man if he gain the whole world, if he loseth his soul?," Will's heart was lifted. It was a solid sermon, delivered with a strong, clear voice, and Will knew the message had to be touching the hearts of the listeners, causing them to remember those values which are eternal. Will thanked God for the ministry of this good man, and for the assurance that he, too, was being given the same sort of opportunity to minister to the spiritual needs of those who had come to the frontier.

At the end of his service, Father Van Gorp introduced Will to the congregation, and Will made the announcement that he would be holding services in this very place at three in the afternoon and again at 8:00 in the evening. He asked those present to pass the word along to those they met during the day, and to assure them that everyone was welcome to come.

Father Van Gorp collected his materials and put them into a valise. Will picked up the priest's single carpetbag of belongings and the two returned to the levee where the incoming boats all docked. In the hour since the *Far West* had landed, the *Nellie Peck* had also come in, having lost its race against the *Far West*. Both vessels had been attempting to set a new speed record in the trip from Sioux City, Iowa, to Fort Benton in the Montana Territory. The *Nellie Peck* had several days' head start, but the *Far West* had finally over-taken and passed her not far downstream from Fort Benton. The *Far West* succeeded in establishing a new speed record for the 1,955 mile journey: 17 days and 20 hours, for an overall speed, going against the current, of around 4.5 miles per hour.

The *Far West*, after many years of notable service, came to the end of her career when she sank in the Missouri River near St. Louis. The cause is not precisely known, but the most logical explanation seems to be that her hull was ripped open when she ran into some debris lodged beneath the surface of the water. For many years, the wreckage could be plainly seen under the water at the foot of Charbonnier Bluff, within sight of old Fort Bellefontaine.

Not long after the *Nellie Peck* arrived, the *Josephine* came into view and tied up at the Fort Benton levee, testimony to

the fact that the river was a busy avenue of commerce at this
time of year. Some years before, in 1866, the *Deer Lodge* had
left Fort Benton on May 20th, bound for St. Louis, and on
her way downstream, before reaching Sioux City she passed
34 ships headed upstream. Even in those early days, the frontier was not such a lonely place as we may have imagined,
especially if one stayed near the waterways.

Prior to the 1860s, travel on the upper Missouri River had
been mainly by man-powered boats such as Lewis and Clark
used at the turn of the century. Prior to 1864 there had been
a total of only 6 steamboat landings at Fort Benton. In 1866
and 1867 there were 70 arrivals. In the year 1867, 40 steamboats had left Sioux City bound for Fort Benton before June
first, carrying more than 12,000 tons of freight, most of it
bound for Fort Benton. Every boat that went upstream also
had to come back down, of course. There wasn't much cargo
flowing downstream, though, except for gold dust. Almost
every boat headed downstream carried some gold. On one
trip in 1866, the *Luella* carried $1,250,000 worth of dust
downriver. Knowledge that the riverboats often carried
substantial quantities of gold made them targets for the bands
of thieves that roamed the plains and added a good bit of
danger and excitement to riverboat travel.

Travel on the river was very seasonal, because the rivers of
the West were not dependably enormous bodies of water, at
least in their upper reaches, and in the months from
September through March or April the rivers were either
frozen or didn't afford enough water for dependable navigation. The Missouri is a considerable stream in the spring,
during a "June rising," but can get rather shallow in places
later in the summer, when the winter snows and spring rains
have all run off. For this reason, the late spring and early
summer were the peak months for the Fort Benton riverboat
trade. Most of the vessels that would go to Montana had to

leave from St. Louis or Sioux City in May or June.

Freight rates for shipping from St. Louis to Fort Benton in 1866 were 12 cents per pound, and insuring the value of the cargo against a possible loss cost from 6½ to 8% of the value of the shipment ($6.50 to $8.00 per hundred dollars). Passenger fare from St. Louis to Fort Benton was $300. The captain of a riverboat usually made around $200 per month, but it was the pilot who commanded top pay. The best ones on the river made $1200 or more per month, for it was understood by all that the safety and survival of the ship, crew, cargo and passengers depended almost totally upon the skill of the pilot.

It was always the custom for riverboats to find a place to tie up to the shore at night. Many military forts were located along the river, and sometimes the boats could tie up in safety at such a place. At other times they had no choice but to tie up in the wilds when darkness fell. True, there was the hazard of a possible Indian attack when they were tied up, but that was considered less of a danger than trying to navigate the river with little or no visibility. The tricky currents caused the sandbars and even the banks of the river to be constantly shifting, and the river was marked from one end to the other with the trunks and complete root systems of large trees, either free-floating, partially lodged as "sawyers" that bobbed up and down in the current, or firmly lodged as "planters" that could stop or sink any ship that ran into them. The steamboat pilots earned their money. It was harrowing, nerve-wracking work avoiding the snags, sandbars and shallows, and there was always the pressure to try to be under way after light had failed in the evening and before it had become light enough in the morning.

Will's journey on the *Far West* occurred during a "June rising." The river was running bank-full due to spring rains and the snow melting in the high mountains as the weather

warmed. The water being deeper, it was indeed a
considerable distance "across the wide Missouri." And with
what may have been more enthusiasm than wisdom, the
captain of the *Far West* decided to depart from the custom of
not traveling at night, hoping to establish a new speed record
on this particular voyage. During the days of Will's journey
upstream, she tied up only for part of one night, and the
passage, luckily, was made safely. The water was high, the
night sky was bright, and for much of the time there was
good moonlight. The pilot could see well enough to navigate
safely, except for part of that one night. As much as he
wanted to set a new speed record, the captain was still aware
of the added risks of night travel, and would not be careless
about the safety of the ship, the cargo, the 40-man crew and
his lone passenger.

When Will and Father Van Gorp reached the levee, the
Roman Catholic priest inquired of the captains of the *Nellie
Peck* and the *Far West* as to their time for departure on the
downstream leg of their run, and whether he could secure
passage. Will told his ship's captain of his good fortune in
finding a place to hold services in the town. All during the
journey, Will had been holding services on the ship for the
crew, and he could have held his final Sunday service aboard
the ship at Fort Benton, but he was eager to make an official
launching of his ministry to those who lived in the West. He
posted a notice on the ship about the services that would be
held in the Powers building that afternoon and evening, and
personally passed the word to those he met.

Now that he was back on the solid footing of the ship's
deck, he noticed that the rain had stopped and it appeared
that the rest of the day might be sunny and fair, as a summer
day should be. He went to the tiny cabin that had been his
home for the past 2½ weeks, sat down on the cot, and
pulled off his muddy boots. The gumbo that had gotten on

his trouser legs was beginning to dry, and he brushed some of it off; the rest would have to wait.

He had a place to preach; now he needed something to say. He had rehearsed this scene in his mind several hundred times, he guessed, in his eager anticipation of the time he would arrive out West. Now that he was actually there, he felt somewhat at a loss. Like many of the people in the East, he had held an image of the people out West as untamed savages. He had already seen enough to know they were anything but that. Those he had met were decent, kind and often well-educated people.

Will reflected on the Sunday morning routine he had grown up with at home, and knew he could be pretty sure what his people were doing at this hour. It occurred to him that everyone out here was in that same situation; they were all immigrants of a sort to this new land. The only natives were the Indians. Everyone else had left home, family, friends and a familiar way of life far behind when they came out west. If they hadn't left their consciousness of God there, too, they had certainly left the public practice of religion. Only now was the church springing to life on the frontier.

Here, perhaps, was the seed of the sermon he would deliver in a few hours. In the Bible was God's promise that He would be with us always. Wherever we may go, He is there, and although we may drift away and lose our consciousness of Him, He does not lose His consciousness of us. Selecting a couple of scripture verses that spoke to this theme, and thinking of several long-familiar hymns that also seemed to fit nicely, Will uttered the silent prayer that God would give him the words to speak. Lying on his cot to think it through, he soon drifted off to sleep. In his excitement at being so near his destination, Will had not been able to sleep much Saturday night as the boat chugged and churned upriver. For most of the trip, the riverboat's sounds had lulled him to sleep, but that last night they had excited him.

Two of the most momentous happenings in the young life of William Wesley Van Orsdel had taken place on the first day of July. It was the day he arrived in Montana and his ministry in the west officially began. It was also the date on which, nine years earlier, the Battle of Gettysburg had begun. That would always be important to Will because he had seen it at close range, some of the combat having taken place on the family farm near the town of Gettysburg. He had heard the sounds of gunfire and the cries of the wounded, and he had seen young men, Union and Confederate, lying dead upon the battlefield. Several months later, he was a member of that assemblage who heard President Abraham Lincoln deliver his now-famous Gettysburg Address.

The youngest of seven children, Will, as his family called him, was born on March 20, 1848. On his father's side, his ancestors were from Holland, making him one of the Pennsylvania Dutch, and no doubt instilling into him some of that noted Dutch stubbornness that he would need in abundance for his eventual career on the frontier in Montana. There it was always easier to give up than to keep going. Will's oft-repeated cry of "Under God, brethren, we must not give up this struggle!" was well known among Montana churchmen, but its roots go back to his Pennsylvania Dutch background. He often said, "Anyone can quit; it takes a man to stay," when a young minister would grow discouraged and want to give up the struggles of establishing a church on the frontier.

His mother's people had come from England, and his grandfather on his mother's side had fought in the Revolutionary War with the Connecticut Colonial Regiment. The roots of patriotism ran just as deep as his Dutch stubbornness, and the Fourth of July was always one of Will's most special holidays. Waving the flag and being in parades would always be important to him.

14

Young Will grew up on a farm, of course, and this would stand him in good stead years later on the Montana frontier. He was a good horseman because of his early experiences, and he was able to relate more effectively to those who were farmers and ranchers due to his early life on the farm, where he learned about hard work, and struggle and privation. He also had learned quite a bit about growing crops and caring for livestock, which was also valuable for his future life on the western frontier.

Will was only ten years old when his father died. Samuel Van Orsdel was a good and devout man who was greatly loved by his family, perhaps most of all by Will, the youngest member of the family. Almost as though she could not bear to continue living without her husband, Will's mother died two years later, and the seven Van Orsdel children became orphans. They were taken by an aunt who lived in the same community, and she gave them all the love and care that a mother would give her own. Three boys and four girls were a major responsibility, even though they were getting to be quite grown up. Will and his two older brothers did the farm work and tried in every way possible to be men upon whom their aunt and their sisters could lean.

Although they had not been permitted to live to see all their children reared to adulthood, Samuel Van Orsdel and his wife had done their job well. Reverence for God and respect for all men was a part of each child's being. In later life, Will said that he could not remember a single occasion when anything had interfered with the family custom of daily prayer and Bible reading, nor could he remember a Sabbath when any sort of circumstances had prevented the family's attendance at the Methodist Church in Gettysburg. This was the church Will joined when he was 12, after he had experienced what he called "a sound conversion to the Lord's side of human affairs."

One of the most lasting impressions and most sacred memories of Will's early life was the death of his favorite sister, just two years older than himself. She had been extremely ill for some time, and the local doctor had been completely unsuccessful in all his attempts to halt the disease that would surely kill the girl. Both the girl's parents were already dead, and as the end of her time was near, she called for Will to be at her side. He was the baby and her favorite. Gripping his hand firmly, she smiled at him feebly as she uttered her last words, "Will, meet me in heaven." Then she was gone, and young Will, pressing her lifeless hand to his face, wept for the third great love he had lost in the past three years. She was laid to rest beside her mother and father, in the community cemetery that was just half a mile from the farm house.

In 1861 when the Civil War began, Will was only 13 years old and too young to fight, but his two older brothers, Samuel and Fletcher, enlisted in the 184th Pennsylvania Regiment and went off to war. This left Will with the responsibilities of operating the farm and being the man of the family for his aunt and three sisters. It was a pretty heavy load for a lad of 13 to bear.

Going to church on the last Sunday evening in June of 1863 promised to be something of special interest. Will and his aunt and sisters never missed attending church services, and on that Sunday morning the pastor had announced that in the Sunday evening service he would be revealing and describing the relative strengths and the positions of the Union and Confederate forces, and would predict events that were soon to follow. He was one of many in that day (and still in this day!) who fancied himself a kind of "armchair general." However successful he may have been in terms of comprehending the battle plans of the two opposing forces, he was extremely successful in getting the attention of his parishioners, and there was a full house for the evening meeting.

After the briefest of services in song, prayer and scripture, the pastor placed a large chalkboard on an easel at the front of the sanctuary and made a rough sketch of the town of Gettysburg and the areas surrounding it on all sides. He wrote in the names of the various unit commanders, with the approximate number of soldiers each one had, at the place on the map where they were believed to be located, awaiting the coming battle.

The minister then gave them what proved to be a remarkably accurate appraisal of the overall situation. "It appears certain the Union and Confederate armies will meet head-on right here at Gettysburg." He tapped his pointer on the board at the spot labeled "Gettysburg," and continued, "We are going to be eyewitnesses to what promises to be one of the major battles of this terrible war. Within the week, we will all have seen war at first hand." In his closing prayer, the pastor pled for the safety of the townspeople, and expressed the hope that the war might soon be over, and that no more lives would be lost. He prayed as well for Will's two brothers and all the other local boys who were in uniform.

How accurate the minister's assessment of the situation had been became evident early on the morning of July first, when the citizens of Gettysburg began to hear distant and yet distinct sounds of field cannons being fired. Speculation ran high as to whose guns were being fired at whom. The local residents, of course, were solidly behind the Union's cause, and the local boys in uniform wore the blue of the Federalist forces.

In spite of stern warnings from his aunt that he should stay in the relative safety of his yard, the intense curiosity of Will and a neighbor boy his age compelled them to engage in a rare act of disobedience. Soon after breakfast the pair left the yard and sneaked in their best Indian fashion to a nearby hilltop where, they hoped, they would be able to get a better idea of what was taking place. All through the day they continued to hear the cannons, and the increasing volume indicated they were drawing nearer. Until late in the afternoon, the two boys were unable to really see anything. It was clear that a battle was in progress, and it annoyed them immensely not to be able to get any idea of what was actually happening. In their fertile and partisan imaginations, they could readily see the Union forces giving the Confederates a severe trouncing.

Then, just as night was beginning to fall, the action moved nearer. The boys were able to see a billow of smoke from a cannon that had been fired, and some seconds later its dreadful sound. Two single cavalrymen and one group of three horsemen came riding furiously through a gap between two hills and disappeared around the side of another hill. Will and his friend agreed the cavalrymen seemed to be wearing the Union blue, but the light was not good enough for them to be certain.

Agreeing that somehow they would get away again the next morning to resume their "advance observer" duties, the two boys went to their homes. Will had a lot of explaining to do, as his aunt was quite upset that he had been gone so long and had left the yard against her orders. Finally he was able to convince her that he and his friend had not been in any danger, and they had no intention of sneaking an inch closer. If she would only let them go and observe the next day, she would know exactly where they were, and they would, in any case, be within shouting distance of the barn. To Will's amazement and delight, his aunt agreed to let them go, with the one condition that if the battle should really come right at them, they would retreat at once to the safety of the house and yard.

When the boys resumed their hilltop vigil very early the next morning, they could see quite clearly much of what was taking place in the valley below and on the surrounding hills. Today there was, at least at this early hour, very little cannon fire. Instead they could see soldiers on foot and on horseback, and hear the crackle of small arms fire. In their youthful excitement, it didn't dawn on them that if they were near enough to see and hear so well, they were too near for their own good. Their attention was riveted upon a contingent of rebel soldiers moving up to launch an attack on a position where a company of Union soldiers was dug in. The two were so engrossed in that unfolding drama that they didn't even hear, until it was too late to retreat, the advance patrol of Confederate horsemen that was coming directly at them. It was the command group of General Jenkins, seeking the best route by which their Confederate forces could attack the Union army which was entrenched on Seminary Ridge.

Jenkins believed them when they told him they were just two local farm boys and that they had no weapons and belonged to no army. They were just innocent and curious bystanders, and nobody had anything to fear on their account. Will pointed out his own house, just a short distance off, and the boys were much relieved when the general told his aides to holster their pistols. Jenkins and his military advisers did their best to get information from the boys as to which slopes were open and which were wooded, and how far it was from various points to other points, and other information they might find helpful. As Union partisans, the two youths did their best to play dumb, and gave Jenkins only such information as anyone could clearly see for himself. Soon the general was convinced that the two country bumpkins were not going to give him anything helpful, so, with an expression of disgust, he ordered his men to ride on.

As the general and his men turned their horses to ride down the next slope, the two youths clearly heard Jenkins commenting to his aides about a Yankee cannon that had been pounding the Confederate positions all morning with unerring accuracy, "That is the most terrible gun in the whole Union army. We must silence it at all costs!"

The two youngsters were relieved when Jenkins left, and were more than a little shaken by the event. They realized, now, they might have been taken captive. It was not at all uncommon for boys of their age to be in uniform. They were also proud of themselves. As scared as they had been, they had not given the Confederates any helpful information. They knew all the hills and valleys, trails and streams in the neighborhood, having romped and played on those hills all their lives, and there was a lot of useful information they could have given General Jenkins, had they felt the least inclination toward abetting the Southern cause.

From their hilltop lookout, it soon became apparent to the boys that Jenkins had meant what he said about silencing that Union cannon. They could observe that the Confederate cannons were all swinging around to aim directly at it, and soon a large contingent of men in gray uniforms could be seen making their way across the valley floor and up the slope of the hill behind which the Union cannon was positioned. They visually followed the rebel soldiers until they went over the crest of the hill and into the Union trenches. Will and his friend, totally caught up in the excitement of the moment, almost literally held their breath as they waited for some sign of what had happened when the Confederates had gone into enemy lines. After what seemed like a very long time, but was probably well under an hour, the roar of the big cannon once again sounded from behind the hill, assuring the boys that their side had prevailed. They surmised that most, if not all, of the Confederate soldiers had been killed or captured in their unsuccessful attempt to put the big gun out of commission.

Communications in wartime are always spotty and unpredictable, and were even more so in the days before the telephone, telegraph and radio. There was no way Will and his family could have known that his brother Fletcher was with the Union forces in the battle in his home town, and that he had been an eyewitness to the now-famed suicide charge of Colonel Pickett's Virginians.

The Battle of Gettysburg seemed to have resulted in a draw, with both sides losing about the same number of men. But somehow, it seemed to be a turning point in the war. After Gettysburg, the South continued to suffer one defeat after another until finally the end for which people had prayed came about as General Lee surrendered to General Grant at Appomattox in Virginia on April 9, 1865.

On November 19, 1865, Will was present when President Abraham Lincoln came to deliver his now-immortal Gettysburg Address. One of his fondest lifelong memories was in getting to shake the President's hand afterward. The entire Civil War experience became an indelible memory to him. Many years later. he developed a lecture which he delivered all over Montana and in a number of other states, titled, "What a Boy Saw and Heard at Gettysburg." Typical of all of these occasions was one reported by the *Hill County Democrat*, when Will delivered that address in Havre, Montana, on February 14, 1914:

> After about two hours of description and story, the audience listened to the singing of our national hymn, and slowly dispersed, congratulating themselves on the opportunity of having listened to one of the greatest lecturers of our day.

Many thousands of lives were lost during the war, both Union and Confederate. But Will's two brothers, Samuel and Fletcher, were among those fortunate enough to return home alive and well. Samuel took over the operation of the farm, while Will, Fletcher and a friend formed an evangelistic team and began holding services in country schools and community halls, and anywhere else they could find a group of people who were not already being served by a regular church. They made up in enthusiasm what they lacked in skill. The major aim of every service they held was that someone present, or more than one, if possible, would decide to commit his or her life to Christ. Will learned early to preach for results, and that meant conversions. Will and Fletcher developed such a firm relationship that they continued to work together in many ways until both were old men. More than brothers, the two were best friends all their lives.

Will made the discovery that there was a genuine hunger for religion among people. He discovered also that those who lived in the more remote and isolated regions were even, more responsive and grateful for the ministry of the young men than were those in the more settled places. No doubt these two discoveries were instrumental in his subsequent decision to go west and practice on a larger scale what he had begun to do in the areas surrounding Gettysburg. Will was already developing a sense of serving on the frontier. In a way, the regions around Gettysburg could be considered a type of frontier, but he knew they were really quite tame and civilized when compared to the true frontier out west. The whole idea of a frontier was to be out there on the edge, where beyond you there is nothing that man has claimed and conquered.

What he had seen during the war, and what he had learned about the war from his brothers, who were both veterans of many battles, had caused Will to mature beyond his years, perhaps. And life had dealt harshly with him in other ways. Before he was 15 years old, he had seen the deaths of his father, mother, and favorite sister, and had been required to assume the role of "man of the house" when his two brothers went off to war. Enduring it had not been easy, but it gave him confidence to assume an adult role on the 3-man evangelistic team, though he was not yet 18 years old when the war ended.

Will, Fletcher and their friend continued their free-lance evangelistic work for nearly six years in the regions surrounding their home. Besides converting quite a number of people to the ways of Christ, and continuously engaging in Bible classes and teaching the ways of Christian living, the young men were gaining valuable experience. To understand the ministry Will developed later in his life, one must take into account the ongoing curriculum in practical experience in which he was immersed for some six years. He began his ministry as he ended it, by exhorting people to come forward, kneel at the altar, and surrender their lives to Christ.

Just before his twenty-third birthday, in March of 1871, Will made a fateful decision. Something, he knew not what, was creating unrest within him. He wasn't able to comprehend any details clearly, but there was something inside him that kept urging him to move westward. He knew that something, or more likely Someone, was calling him toward some great and special objective, and that he had no choice but to follow the demands of that voice, wherever it might lead him.

With the advent of better weather in the spring, and the roads drying up enough that travel was not too difficult, Will pointed himself West. At Oil City, Pennsylvania, two hundred miles west of Gettysburg, his money ran out. He was homeless, penniless and jobless before he had even made a good start on heading for the West. But he knew he could always rely upon that inner voice that kept prodding him along. If God wanted him so badly to get out West, He would do whatever it would take to allow it to happen.

Before that day was out, he had two solid proofs that God was still standing by and was opening the doors that needed to be opened for him. That very day, he secured a job as operator of a stationary engine which pumped oil from a well. Then, on the strength of his employment, he was able to find a rooming-house proprietress who agreed to give him room and board on credit until his first payday. Only hours after arriving in town, he was no longer homeless, penniless or jobless.

In the first hour Will was on his new job, it appeared he might not keep it. His boss was more than a little upset when Will told him he could not work on Sunday. Everyone else in the oil fields worked seven days a week, and if there had been anyone else around that he could have hired, the oilman would have cheerfully fired Will on the spot. Not having a replacement, he agreed to let Will have Sundays off, on the condition that he would have to pump as much oil in 6 days as all the others pumped in 7 days from wells that were known to produce at the same rate as Will's well. Having no choice, Will accepted the challenge, and surprised himself and everyone else by being able to win his Sabbath holiday each week.

He always tried to be the first one in the morning to reach his pumphouse and get the engine going, and the last to shut it off at night. Most of the other men who operated engines would get their engines started and then join in one of the pumphouses for a game of cards. While they were playing cards, an engine would sometimes stop, and it would take a little while to get it started again, even if a man noticed at once when it died. Will watched his engine like a hawk and was able to keep it running at full force all day every day. He was always able to pump more oil than any of the other operators on any given day, and surprised his supervisor by making good on his promise to pump more oil from his well in six days than the others could pump in seven.

Will was strict and totally unbending in his observance of the Sabbath, and remained so all his life. It was a day of rest and of prayer. That meant going to church at least in the morning and evening, and it meant doing no work, nor doing anything that caused anyone else to work. (So far as we know, he was not opposed to eating on Sunday, nor the work that preparing meals required of the women.) He would have quit his job of pumping oil if he had been told that he had to work on Sundays.

From March until August, Will tended his stationary engine from daylight to dark six days a week. The seventh day was spent, as it had been back home in Gettysburg, in free-lance evangelistic work. Oil City was a newly-established town, typical of the brawling new oil industry, and there was little of civil or divine law observed there. There were no churches and no regular religious services being held by anyone. The usual custom seemed to be that when people got off work in the oil fields, they merely transferred their card games from the pumphouses to one of the town's numerous saloons. It seemed to Will as though there were lots of people around there who needed to let God direct their paths into some new ways.

Will's evangelistic work met with good success. He met quite a number of interested people, and his Sunday services were always very well-attended when he preached at various places in the surrounding country. After working for about 5 months as a stationary engineer, Will quit his job and went to work full-time as a preacher. He had no official status, nor the support of any denomination, but he was not deterred by those trifles. In this and in many later endeavors, he operated on the simple principle that if God wanted that work done, He would provide the means to see that it was accomplished.

It was a bright and sunny August morning when the new pastor of the Oil City parish started on his rounds to visit his parishioners. Not knowing where it would be best to begin, he started walking, and soon found himself at the Shaw farm, three miles outside of Oil City. Several of the better oil wells of the area were located on the Shaw place, and Will decided to call on some of the engine operators. They were almost all people he knew, and he also knew their trade, so he could speak their language in terms of their work.

The first pumphouse he approached was the one where he had worked. He was interested in meeting the person who had been hired to replace him. He discovered there a young man, about his own age, who was busily oiling and checking his engine. Will could tell he would be an excellent operator. Extending his hand in greeting, Will said, "Good morning! How goes it, brother?"

Young Tommy Rogers was surprised by the intrusion, and knew better than to speak with strangers. He had just arrived from the East a short time before, and had been sternly warned by his mother, as he left home, that he would have to beware of "confidence men" out on the frontier. Such men, she had been told, were numerous, and they would rob and kill people with little reason and with no remorse. Tommy, remembering his mother's warnings, turned his back on Will, refusing to accept the proffered hand. Awkwardly, Will retracted his outstretched hand, and made another approach to opening a conversation with the young man. Tommy wouldn't budge. Will couldn't have gotten the time of day out of him, much less any meaningful conversation, so he left quickly, after saying, "Well, good day to you."

Tommy was staying in Oil City at the home of his older

brother and family. That night at the dinner table, Tommy
said, "One of those confidence men came to my pumphouse
today to see me, but he wasted his time on me. I froze him
out so badly, I'll bet he leaves me alone from now on." This
interested the elder Rogers brother. He had been around Oil
City about as long as anyone, and knew everyone in town.
He said to Tommy, "There are for sure a few unsavory
people around here. The oil fields seem to attract them like
flies. If you can give me a good description of this menacing
character who approached you, I may be able to figure out
who it was."

Tommy began, and before he had gotten far into his
description, his brother began to laugh uproariously. He
could barely gasp the words through his laughter, "Do you
know who it was you froze out, Tommy? It was Brother Van
Orsdel, the only pious young man in this entire settlement!
He's the one person in this oil field you absolutely could
trust to do you no harm." As it happened, Tommy had also
heard about Brother Van Orsdel, but hadn't been in the right
place at the right time to meet him as yet. His feeling of
triumph at having stopped the "confidence man" in his tracks
turned to one of chagrin, for Tommy was also a pious young
man. He had been kept very close to the church back home,
and his family, like Will's, never missed Sunday services, nor
any other extra meetings that were held at the church or in
the community. Tommy said to his brother, "Now, I've just
got to find this man and meet him properly, and apologize
for my bad behavior when he came to call on me."

As good as his word, Tommy asked around until he found
out where Brother Van Orsdel would be preaching the next
Sunday, and made it a point to be present, even though
getting there involved a walk of several miles from his
brother's home.

Will was surprised to see in the congregation that Sunday

morning the same young man who had treated him so rudely only a few days before in the oilfield pumphouse. After the service, Tommy hung around until everyone else had gone, and then he introduced himself to the minister. "Brother Van Orsdel, I'm Tommy Rogers, and I must apologize to you for my poor treatment of you when you came to see me in the oilfield a few days ago."

"I recognized you at once," Will said, his blue eyes twinkling with mirth, "but no apologies are necessary. It may not have been in good taste for me to have dropped in on you at work, unannounced."

"Oh, that part of it was no problem at all. You see, when I left home, my mother lectured me at length about how I had to watch out for what she called 'confidence men' who were fast talkers and would like to get their hands on whatever money I had. Dressed as you were, I thought you could have been one. I knew you weren't a farmer or an oilfield worker."

Always able to enjoy a good joke, even if it was at his own expense, Will laughed heartily when he heard the explanation for Tommy's behavior. "I don't blame you a bit, Tommy. You were right not to be too trusting of just anyone who may walk up to you. Out here on the edge of civilization there are some bad types you don't want to get mixed up with. But now that you know I'm safe to talk to, tell me about yourself, where you've been and where you're going in life."

It proved to be the inauspicious beginning of a firm, lifelong friendship. Tommy became one of the most active supporters of the evangelistic work Will was doing in the Oil City region, and was a staunch churchman. He became a preacher and thus twice as many services could be held. He and Will maintained a correspondence for the next 40 years, and when Will, very late in his career, issued a special call for workers to come to the North Montana Mission, Tommy sold his business in Pennsylvania and came to Montana to labor beside his old friend. In Will's later journals and letters, there are occasional references to "Rev. Tommy Rogers." Tommy and Fletcher Van Orsdel were appointed to serve as evangelists-at-large in the North Montana Mission, of which Will was for many years the superintendent.

After Will and Tommy teamed up, the evangelistic work around Oil City gained momentum. The two held preaching services anywhere a tiny handful of people could be found. Sites such as Shaw's farm, Oleopolis, Oak Grove and Walnut Bend became preaching points for them, and there were both immediate and long-term results of their efforts. It is known that Walnut Bend, where services were held in a school-house, produced three young men who became Methodist ministers.

In the total parish, it was not long until there had been over a hundred conversions—easily enough to formally organize a Methodist Church, Will thought, and the people agreed. Before Will had quit his job in the pumphouse and started holding evangelistic services, it would have been impossible to find 100 people in the area who would have voted in favor of going to church on Easter, and now there were more than 100 clamoring for the establishment of their own real church.

The Methodist denominational officials were delighted, of course, to have a new Methodist congregation chartered, and it was only to be expected that the Oil City congregation implored Will to become the first pastor of the new congregation. They offered him free room and board plus the then-princely sum of $800 per year in salary. It didn't take Will long to come up with his response to their offer. His voice trembled at times as he spoke, and his eyes brimmed with tears of tenderness and gratitude. "I appreciate this kind and generous offer more than I can say. In the few months that we have been working here, I have come to know and love you dear folks, and I know that if I stayed, we would have some glorious times together in the Lord's work.

"But there is a voice inside me, calling, pleading with me to go way out west. I'm not sure what awaits me there, but it is clear to me it is the voice of God, and I cannot be disobedient to that heavenly vision. It is going to be spring very soon now, and I must continue my journey westward. Believe me, I will never forget you, and Oil City will always be my second home. You folks helped me to learn to walk as a young minister. This church and community and you dear friends will always have a special place in my heart."

About two weeks later, Will and a young man about his own age from the new Oil City Methodist Church traveled to Chicago. The two young men were to have a few days' vacation in the great city. The friend would return to his work at Oil City, and Will would make the rounds to say goodbye at Oil City and then go on to Gettysburg for a few days before his western journey. On their first night in the city, the two went to hear a widely-noted lecture, "The Bright Side of Life in Libby Prison." The lecturer, Chaplain McCabe, a chaplain in the Union Army during the Civil War, had been taken captive by the Confederacy and incarcerated in the infamous Libby Prison.

The tales the chaplain told of his adventures during the war and his captivity were spine-tingling, but what made the evening truly memorable was that Will and his friend went backstage after the lecture and were able to have a short conversation with the noted speaker. Will's companion explained to the Chaplain how their minister had declined an urgent invitation to remain as pastor in Oil City in favor of going out West. McCabe's reply became indelibly etched in Will's memory, and cemented forever his decision to proceed to the West: "Go away out west and you will realize what Paul meant when he said he rejoiced he did not build on any man's foundation. You will find few foundations out there!"

Now, in Will's mind, the vision that had been calling to him began to assume intelligible form. Later, he wrote of that impression that he felt compelled to respond to the mighty vision. He said "away out on the frontier and even to the summit of the Rockies, I could see the miners, stage drivers, freighters, cowboys, and . . . copper-colored natives, holding up their hands and beckoning. I could see their tears falling, and their whole being reaching out for the religion of their childhood. . .To me these were Macedonian cries, and with the all-impelling word 'Go' locked up like fire in my bones, I felt like Paul: 'Woe be unto me if I go not' and thus hearken to the appeal made by the Holy Spirit."

In testimony to the accuracy of the words of Chaplain McCabe and their impact on the young preacher, one needs only to read a short while in Will's journals of later years. Time and again he makes note of the fact that this was the first church service held, the first wedding, the first baptism, the first church organized, or the first Christian burial in a certain community. He seemed almost obsessed with the notion that he was an instrument in building the Kingdom from the ground up out on the frontier, and that he was building on no other man's foundations. He was doing what had never been done before.

Due to his simple and modest style of living, Will had been able to save a substantial fraction of what he had earned from his work in the oil fields and as a pastor in Oil City. After he heard Chaplain McCabe deliver his stirring lecture and had the conversation with him, his mind was made up beyond any shadow of doubt—he would go to the far west to continue his ministry. The decision normally would have been a hard one to make, and logic would have been on the side of remaining in Oil City. But for Will it was easy to see he really had no choice but to follow the vision that was leading him west.

Will was eager to go home and see his family and friends for a few final days. As planned, he stopped for a couple of days at Oil City and bade goodbye to Tommy Rogers and many other friends, and to his newly-formed classes in the region. He knew it was unlikely he would be able to return home again very soon, and some of his relatives and friends he would probably never see again, so this final visit assumed much importance to him.

As he spoke with friends and family members back home in Gettysburg, most people had difficulty understanding why he was so drawn toward the farthest frontiers. To just travel through a wilderness largely uninhabited except for hostile Indians seemed bad enough in itself; to willingly go and live in such a Godforsaken place was unthinkable, and to even give consideration to staying there for years and years went far beyond unthinkable.

After a pleasant but all too brief visit with his family and friends in and around Gettysburg, at the first hint that spring was just around the corner, he purchased a one-way train ticket from Gettysburg to Chicago to Sioux City, and bade his loved ones farewell.

Of his departure a few days later, he wrote, "I did not feel worthy to ask for help from the Missionary Society nor from anybody else, but with a very small amount of money in my pocket, started." As travelers from time immemorial have done, he underestimated what his travels would cost, and arrived in Sioux City in the same condition in which he'd arrived at Oil City—homeless, jobless and penniless. He was dismayed to learn that his future funds would also disappear rather quickly, because prices on the frontier had been spiraling upward recently. There was enormous demand for the goods and services that could be brought to the frontier, and, of course, high demand translated into high prices, then as now. Riverboat freight charges had practically quintupled in the past four or five years, rising from around two cents per pound to about 12 cents. Most other costs had similarly increased, he learned, by as much as three or four times what they had been just five years earlier.

With the abandon characteristic of youth, Will paid scant attention to the reports of dangers and difficulties encountered by those who traveled west. To him, it sounded much more exciting than dangerous. If only half of what he had heard proved to be true, he was in for some real excitement. People not only had harrowing adventures, but delighted in telling of them, and most tellers of frontier tales, he knew, were not reluctant to add some fitting embellishments. While he knew he was walking deliberately into certain hardships and possible danger, Will chose to ignore those aspects, perhaps in the belief that if he was going out West on God's business, it was God's responsibility to see that he got there with his scalp intact.

The rail lines connecting Chicago with Sioux City, Iowa, had just been completed three or four years earlier. Until then, St. Louis had been the most common jumping-off place for those heading west. Being able to board a riverboat at Sioux City instead of at St. Louis reduced the length of the boat trip by about a thousand miles. Traveling only in daylight hours, Missouri River steamships typically made only about 50 miles a day. Thus, a reduction of 1000 miles would have amounted to roughly 20 days of travel saved.

Having nowhere else to turn, Will asked at the train station how he could find the local Methodist Church, knowing the parsonage would be next door, and that he would almost certainly find a ready welcome with a fellow pastor. He was right. He found the Reverend and Mrs. Cozier at home, and upon introducing himself to them as a fellow member of the Methodist clergy, they received him gladly and invited him to remain with them for whatever period of time it would be until he found passage up the river to the Montana Territory.

In presenting himself to the Coziers as a fellow Methodist minister, Will was, in a way, stretching the truth just a little. Actually, he had undertaken no ministerial studies, and had never been ordained as a clergyman by the Methodist denomination. If he were to have taken regular employment as a Methodist minister somewhere in the east, he would have had to either attend seminary or embark upon what is called the "conference course of study." Those are the two possible avenues by which a person comes into the Methodist ministry. Since Will had been working as a free-lance evangelist who happened himself to be a Methodist, he was certainly not engaging in any wrongdoing. He just wasn't really and officially a Methodist minister yet. This did not trouble Will, nor did it trouble the denominational officials. The declaration and demonstration of an earnest intent carried more weight than did ordination.

No doubt the main and only reason Will had not sought official clerical status is just that he was too busy doing his evangelistic work, starting classes, and holding revivals to have time for seminary or seminary studies. Throughout his life he was a person to whom an active and practical demonstration of the faith meant more than going through official, formal motions. Had he sought formal affiliation, he could have asked for help from the Methodist Mission Society, and, in all probability, they would have paid for his travel from Pennsylvania to the Montana Territory. Knowing he was not officially a Methodist minister yet, he felt unworthy to seek such help, and so was reduced to having to work and beg his way to Montana.

During his stay with the Coziers, Will made himself useful

by helping the pastor with his calling, assisting (usually leading) in the song services at the church, and even preaching on a couple of occasions. He especially enjoyed the Wednesday evening services, because there was so much music in them. He rendered for them a few special selections, some of the Moody-Sankey revival songs that were so popular at the time. His rich, strong voice had a unique power to stir the hearts of those who heard him sing. It would become a legend on the frontier, and was well on its way to becoming a legend in Sioux City by the time his brief stay there was ending.

So well-liked was the young Pennsylvanian that great inducements were held out, as they had been in Oil City, to entice him to relinquish his plans for going to the far frontier and remain in Iowa. The Methodist Presiding Elder, the Reverend Bennett Mitchell, made Will a tantalizing offer, but nothing fired his spirit as did the thought of going out West. There was no offer anyone could make which would be sufficient to deter him from his course. To all their most urgent appeals he made the same sincere response, "I sincerely appreciate your asking me to stay here and work; your offers are most generous and kind. But the voice of duty to me seems clear, calling me far beyond here, to the line of the mountains. Woe be unto me if I fail to heed the heavenly vision."

When he was not otherwise engaged, Will haunted the waterfront area, hoping to find a vessel bound for the head of navigation—Fort Benton in the Montana Territory. His frequent inquiries were rewarded one day in June with the news that the sternwheeler the *Far West* had come into port, and was now beginning to load the cargo that would be delivered to various forts and settlements upstream, with Fort Benton its final destination. He found the vessel easily enough, and approached a man standing on the wharf, supervising the loading operation. It proved to be the ship's captain, Martin Coulson. Coulson was a veteran Missouri River pilot. The *Far West* was a nearly-new steamship, having been launched in 1870, but Coulson had piloted other vessels for a number of years.

Captain Coulson knew it was important for him to supervise the loading of nearly 400 tons of freight, because on the Missouri River, particularly in its upper reaches, it was critical that the front of the ship be more heavily loaded than the back. If the rear portion of the ship were more heavily-loaded than the front, the ship's nose would ride high in the water, making it possible for a snag or other debris to go far under the ship, and thus perhaps to lodge the vessel so firmly that nothing could free it to get moving again. With the front end loaded more heavily, the bow would be lower in the water, and would run afoul of any possible snag before the ship actually ran over it and risked the possibility of getting stuck. When the ship was front-heavy, anything deep enough for the bow to clear was deep enough for the entire vessel to clear. Besides the weight distribution, there was also the problem that items which would be unloaded first had to be placed where they could be readily found when their destination was reached. To accomplish all of that required skilled planning, and the overall success of the journey was very closely related to the manner in which the cargo was loaded.

Upon his inquiry about the ship's departure, Will learned that the *Far West* was scheduled to cast off at noon the next day, the 12th of June. Many of the steamships on the river were veritable floating luxury hotels, and to take a trip on such a vessel was certainly to travel first class. The *Far West*, however, was a cargo vessel, and had cabins only for its own crew and few, if any, others. For this particular trip, as it happened, there would be room for just one person besides the crew.

In his impoverished condition, Will was reluctant to ask
Captain Coulson what the fare would be from Sioux City to
Fort Benton. No matter what sum Coulson might name, it
would be more than he had, for his pockets were still as
empty as they had been upon his arrival. During his few
weeks as the Coziers' guest, he had performed a variety of
ministerial chores in exchange for his room and board. He
had received no cash salary, nor did he expect any. His hosts
had been exceedingly kind and generous to him, and he was
grateful.

Finally, of course, he was forced to ask what the fare to
Fort Benton would be. Captain Coulson informed him that
the usual fare for the 1,955-mile trip was one hundred
dollars. On this particular trip, there would be so much cargo
aboard that there would be space for only one person extra.
In view of that, the captain said Will could go with them for
a reduced fee of seventy-five dollars. As an afterthought,
Captain Coulson inquired, "Why are you going to Montana,
son?"

"To sing and preach, and encourage the people to be
good," was Will's prompt reply.

"In all my years of running this river," Coulson said, "I've
taken a lot of folks for a lot of different reasons, but I've
never taken anyone before who was going to Montana for
that reason." After a moment's thought, the captain said,
"Tell you what, son. If you will agree to do a little singing
and preaching on the *Far West*, and encourage my crew to
be good, I'll take you to Fort Benton for only $50." Captain
Coulson was asking him, Will understood, to be a sort of
chaplain for the vessel during its voyage, holding Sunday
services and having some hymn-singing at various times.

Will recognized this as an exceptional offer, but he knew
that before he went any further he would have to tell the
Captain about his lack of funds. Rather than pleading poverty

directly, Will said that if it were possible to defer payment of the fifty dollars, Coulson would find it waiting for him at the Methodist Church upon his return to Sioux City. Martin Coulson was tempted to call the whole thing off, having seen his share of scams pulled by confidence men. But there was something so right, so intent, and so earnest about this stocky young dutchman that the Captain found himself agreeing to accept this bizarre arrangement, despite his better judgment.

Will felt no guilt, for in his own mind he was not being dishonest. True, he had no arrangements with anyone who had promised to come forth with the money, but he felt certain he was telling Captain Coulson the truth—the money would be in Sioux City waiting for him. And it was! Nobody ever revealed the source of the gift, whether it had been collected by the members of Pastor Cozier's flock, or was arranged for by the presiding elder through the Methodist Mission Society, or had been contributed by an anonymous donor. Wherever it came from, it was there. Captain Coulson promptly sent most of it to Will in Montana, having grown fond of the young preacher during their voyage up the Missouri River.

Having made the travel arrangements that would actually land him in Montana, Will was as excited as he had ever been in his twenty-four years. He couldn't wait to get back to the parsonage to tell the Coziers of his good fortune. In the few weeks Will had been in Sioux City, he and the Coziers had become close friends. In honor of his last night with them, Mrs. Cozier suggested that Will and her husband should get busy spreading the word around town that there would be an open house all evening at the parsonage. That night a good many people from the church and from all over town came by to say goodbye to Will, and to wish him a good journey.

It was after eleven by the time the last guests had departed. Tired as he was, Will was too excited to sleep soundly, and he was up early the next morning. Packing his belongings was not an exacting or time-consuming task. Besides the clothes he wore, he had a few extra items of clothing, his Bible and song books, and little else. He was ready to go, pacing the floor, with several hours to spare before the noon-time departure.

About eleven o'clock he and the Coziers walked the short distance to the waterfront. The pastor and his wife went on board and saw the little room that would be Will's quarters for the next two or three weeks. The three exchanged small talk and gave occasional greetings to the crew members who passed by, and finally, as twelve o'clock came, Captain Coulson called out, "All ashore that's going ashore!" Mrs. Cozier gave Will a warm hug and kissed him on the cheek. "We've come to love you, Will, in your short stay with us, and we pray you have a safe journey. If you ever come back down the river, be sure to come and see us. And write when you can." Pastor Cozier shook Will's hand vigorously as he seconded his wife's words, and he added, "I know that God is with you, Will, and that you will be doing mighty works for Him in Montana. I pray for him to guide and bless you always. Farewell, my dear friend."

As Captain Coulson issued the second call, the visitors stepped off the sternwheeler, and the order was given to cast off the mooring lines. The *Far West's* bow swung into the current as the paddlewheel churned the murky water of the Missouri. Ever so slowly, the figures on the wharf began to recede into the distance, and Will knew that, at last, he was on the way to Montana and the realization of his dreams. While he had been at Sioux City, Will had made some short forays along the riverbank, so the territory through which they passed during the first couple of hours was familiar to him. Will used this time to explore the boat and to get acquainted with some of the crewmen. The cabin boy was a pleasant young man named Jack, whom Will liked at once. Each crew member had specific tasks to do in keeping the ship going. Jack was to clean and care for the crew members' rooms, leaving them free to do their assigned duties. Will's duties, like those of Jack, were in the nature of service to the crew instead of having anything to do with the actual operation of the vessel. As a "paying" passenger, he had time to just stand around and observe all that was going on aboard the ship and on the shore.

Will was overjoyed to learn some years later that Jack had left the river to become a minister. No doubt there had also been other forces at work upon the young man, but Will liked to think that impressions made during the journey from Sioux City to Fort Benton in June of 1872 had been the major impetus. Jack was the most spiritually-minded member of the crew, and he assisted Will in getting song and prayer sessions going on board the *Far West.*

Here, as it had been in other places, Will saw that one of the best avenues for gaining the interest and attention of people was to get them singing. Almost everyone, he found, had some favorite song from home and childhood, and some remembrances of church, the Bible, and prayer. The shipboard services were kept very brief and informal, and Will seldom actually launched into a sermon. Instead, he interspersed between the songs bits of quiet testimony about the nature, quality and value of the Christian life. It was probably the most effective kind of preaching and evangelizing that could be done in such a setting. Captain Coulson and the crew members, as well as Will himself, came to look forward to this pleasant time at the close of each day. It helped them to put a proper perspective on their life and labor.

The first night out from Sioux City, Will slept long and
peacefully, only occasionally arousing to an awareness that
the ship was still chugging and churning its way up the great
river. The sounds he could hear included those of the
crewmen on night duty, stoking the hungry furnaces with
wood, producing the steam which turned the great
paddlewheel at the stern. Other crewmen were on watch,
peering into the darkness to discern if any hazards lay ahead.
Traveling upriver by night was so dangerous that it was
seldom practiced. If the sky was clear and the moon was out,
it helped enormously; in that early day there were no
headlights or floodlights that could penetrate the darkness. By
the end of their watch at night, the crew members who were
the lookouts were exhausted from their hours of total
tension.

When Will came out of his cabin the next morning, he
could see that some definite progress had been made during
the night; the countryside through which they were now
passing was unfamiliar. The pastoral landscapes around Sioux
City had given way to a more open, prairie-like country.
Hillsides were dotted with clumps of sagebrush as they
sloped gently away from the river's edge. The riverbank, in
most places, was sparsely wooded, but occasionally there
were areas of fairly extensive woodlands. On these the riverboats depended for the supply of wood to feed their
ravenous furnaces. In this spring season, the vegetation was
lush and green as far as one could see. Later, with the cessa-
tion of the spring rains and the advent of summer's heat, all
would be sere and brown except the areas near the water.

As he studied the unfamiliar landscape, Will suddenly
gasped in astonishment and cried out, "Look! On that hillside
to the north! It's an Indian battle!" Warriors were dashing
this way and that on their horses, attacking and being
attacked, so that it was impossible to count them, but Will

estimated there must have been close to a hundred combatants. Will couldn't bear to watch the conflict any longer, after he saw several men fall from their horses, having been struck by enemy arrows or lances. It was altogether too real, a small-scale replay of what he had seen at Gettysburg just a few years before, and he had no stomach for such deadly violence.

A veteran crewman told the tenderfoot preacher that such sights were not uncommon in this region. The Yankton Sioux were constantly having to defend their rich ancestral hunting grounds from those who envied them and wished to steal it. The fertile grasslands were a haven for buffalo and other game, and there were many who were willing to risk life and limb to obtain so great a prize.

The question arose in Will's mind: if we are in hostile country just one day's travel from Sioux City, what is it going to be like when we really get into the wilderness? The battle passed over the hill and out of sight, and as the ship's crew went to breakfast in the galley, little else was talked of than the battle, and there was much speculation about its outcome. It seemed likely to Will that a day would come, perhaps soon, when he would be compelled to play some role other than spectator in such a conflict. He was right.

The *Far West's* three furnaces consumed prodigious amounts of fuel in creating the steam which turned the great paddlewheel at its stern. It was necessary, almost every day, to pull ashore at a cottonwood grove and take on board a new supply of fuel. The steamboat companies had hired crews of woodcutters who worked at several points along the river, readying wood for the ships that would stop. Some early-day entrepreneurs worked in certain places as free-lance woodcutters, selling the produce of their labors to ships that needed it, and there were a good many. The woodcutters felled trees and cut them into the lengths required by the ships' furnaces. The wood was piled by the landing site so it could be loaded quickly once the ship had stopped. In this way, a minimum amount of time was lost in refueling, and more miles could be made each day. The main business of the steamboats was to get up and down the river as quickly as possible.

In the more distant upper reaches of the river, they found that in some places the Indians had killed or driven off the woodcutting crews. At those refueling stops, it was necessary for the ship's crew, perhaps after burying the remains of one or more woodmen, to cut their own wood. To avoid spending too much time ashore, the trees were cut into pieces as large as the men could possibly carry, and load them on the boat as quickly as possible. They would be cut into stove lengths while the ship was under way.

Long delays ashore were not only costly in terms of lost travel time, but also exposed the ship and crew to added dangers. Marauders, both red and white, knew that the ships had to go ashore periodically for fuel and were easy targets at such times. It was also common knowledge, of much more interest to the white men than the Indians, that vessels going downstream often carried substantial amounts of gold. Since the *Far West* was headed upstream, there was little likelihood of any attacks by white bandits. Wood-gathering parties were usually routine and uneventful, but that was not always the case.

One day a large cottonwood grove came into view, and Captain Coulson decided it would be a good time to replenish the ship's wood supply. There were no company or free-lance woodcutters stationed here, but there was an abundant wood supply which the crew could cut. On a hillside about half a mile away a few Indians could be seen stalking some deer. They seemed intent on their hunting and the captain considered them no threat as he ordered the ship to tie up for wood-gathering. The minute the gangplank was in place, the thicket erupted with Sioux in full war regalia who had cleverly used the hunters as decoys. The Indians began to board the ship, and the *Far West's* crew, greatly outnumbered, had the good sense to offer no resistance. The warriors explored the ship, looking for items of interest and value, but found little that appealed to them. Captain Coulson, with great tact and courage, tried to communicate with their leaders, but was handicapped by knowing only a few simple words of greeting in the Indians' tongue. After some anxious moments, the Sioux either decided to leave or were persuaded to by the offer of a handful of trinkets and a few slabs of bacon, and the riverboat quickly pulled away from shore and resumed its upstream course.

Will more fully appreciated the danger they had all been in when he was informed by one of the veteran riverboaters that two of the Sioux Indians who had so recently stood on the deck of the *Far West* were Sitting Bull and Rain-in-the-Face, the mention of whose names was guaranteed to send chills down the back of all on the frontier. How easily they could have taken the ship and its contents and killed or captured all the crew! And how strange that they had done no harm, after all the trouble they had gone to in order to set the trap that enabled them to board the vessel. Will took it as another sign that God's hand was in his westward journey, and believed that he had been spared again from possible danger by the fact that God had great things in mind for the young preacher from Pennsylvania.

Will always joined in the wood-gathering forays, helping with any and all aspects of the process, including loading the heavy pieces on the ship. Sometimes it was he who drew the duty of climbing a nearby hill to serve as a lookout, in hope of preventing a surprise attack while the riverboat was tied up at shore.

As the *Far West* churned her way against the current of the mighty Missouri, almost every day presented some interesting, exciting and memorable event. Although it seemed to Will that this journey of over 1,950 miles was taking forever, the captain assured him they were, in fact, making very good time, and stood the chance of setting a new speed record for the trip. The sameness of the scenery that passed by so slowly day after day early in the trip more than convinced Will that the Great Plains were aptly named. He could not help but be impressed with the vastness of this western country, and his eagerness to explore it grew with every passing day.

One of the most startling and haunting experiences of the whole trip came on a day as they neared the end of their journey. The steamship drove past a group of Indians camped near the river's edge, and those on board the ship could plainly see that in the encampment were two white women and several white children. Since the Indians were well-armed and had horses on which to ride if they were chased, and the ship's crew had neither, there was really nothing they could do to come to the aid of the white captives. How had this come about? What would be their fate? Since they were still alive now, it seemed reasonable to assume the captives would be more or less well-treated. Of course everyone tried to figure out what kind of happening could account for the presence of the white women and children in the Indian camp. The most widely-accepted supposition was that these people were probably the sole survivors of a wagon train that had been raided by the Indians. Perhaps the Indian tribe took them because they had at the time a short supply of women and children. They never did learn the answer to that riddle, nor did they ever hear of the outcome of the white people's captivity.

Had those on board the *Far West* been tourists, they

would have gotten far more than their money's worth in terms of awe-inspiring vistas and panoramas. Most of the more spectacular sights were encountered during the last week of the trip, as they came nearer to the end of the navigable waters of the Missouri. Here, the river often passed through deep-cut canyons of multi-colored rock and clay. In the country known as "the Missouri breaks," the effects of ages of weathering could be seen. Outcroppings and spires of varied and unusual shapes were on every hand. Cliffs were often high and precipitous, and the bottom lands along the river, as well as the hills sloping up from its shores, were often heavily wooded in scrub pines and junipers. The land appeared literally to teem with buffalo and other wild game, while the waterways sheltered great numbers of ducks, geese and other birds. The nearer they came to their destination, the more Will's fascination with the land grew. He had not yet really set foot on Montana soil, except for a few wood-cutting stops, but he had already fallen in love with the place. Many years later, he would remark to a friend who announced his intention to leave Montana and go to work in some more safe and settled place, "Brother, to me Montana is next to heaven, and I'm not leaving Montana until I go straight up!"

Fort Benton was, by now, almost literally just around the bend, Captain Coulson assured his anxious passenger. "I figure we should pull in sometime early Sunday morning, if all continues to go well."

There was still a little more than a full day's journey ahead of them, and it would be necessary, one more time, to take on a supply of wood. As they approached the final wood-yard, no woodcutters could be seen, but instead there stood a lone frontiersman, clad from head to foot in the finest buckskin suit Will had ever seen. It was white and had fringes on the shirt sleeves and all down the sides of the trousers. The man cradled a huge rifle in his arm as he flagged the boat into the landing. Before they had fully reached the shore, Jim Dexter jumped aboard and shouted to the captain, whom he had met on several other occasions at Fort Benton, "Let's get out of here, Mart! There's too many hostiles around here to suit me!"

Dexter, a mountain man, trapper and hunter, was the first real Montanan Will had met, and he could not help but be impressed with the man and his bearing. Will was eager to engage him in conversation, but the captain had other plans for the immediate future. They would still have to find a place before long to get some wood, but he knew Dexter was as good as his word: if he said there was danger near at hand, it would be foolish not to heed the warning. They were also in need of some wild game. Coulson said, knowing that Dexter was reputed to be one of the finest marksmen in all Montana, "Jim, do you reckon you could bring down a deer for us? We're about down to our last meal of fresh meat, and there's a small herd grazing near the riverbank, just ahead on your right."

In wordless answer to the request, Dexter stepped over to the ship's rail, raised his rifle and fired. To Will it didn't even appear the man had bothered to aim the weapon, but one of the deer dropped, shot cleanly in the neck. Captain Coulson ordered a boat to be lowered to go ashore and bring the deer back to the ship to be dressed out. The crewmen were eager to go, already savoring the delicious venison chops they would soon be eating. But just as the boat was about to touch water, the "hostiles" of whom Dexter had spoken were seen hiding in the brush along the shore. "Hold it, boys. We'll bring you back aboard the ship. I guess we weren't hungry for any fresh venison right now, after all." The Indians, he knew, would make good use of the fresh venison and the hide; the animal would not be wasted.

Later the same day they were hailed by another frontiersman who was standing at another of the places where
riverboats often stopped for fuel. Beside him was his white
companion-interpreter, and a group of four Indians. He
assured them it was safe to come ashore, and when they had
secured the boat, he came aboard and introduced himself as
Bill Cody. "Buffalo Bill" was then in his prime, age 26, just 2
years older than Will, and he had already established such a
good reputation with the Indians that he could go anywhere
on the plains in safety. They trusted him to do them no
harm, and he never betrayed them.

Will wished that he and all the rest could have similar
immunity, for the events of the past couple of weeks had
convinced him that the frontier land to which he had come
was often a dangerous and violent place. He understood and
felt a great deal of sympathy for the Indians' position. They
saw the white men as invaders of their private domain, and
they had a right to defend their homelands and their hunting
grounds. But, it also seemed that the white settlers had a right
to come out West and harness some of its vast resources. To
Will it seemed that it should be possible for them to come to
a fair agreement that would allow them to live together on the
frontier in peace and harmony. Until such an accord was
struck, both red men and white would continue to live in fear
and distrust, and many people would die.

While Buffalo Bill and Captain Coulson talked, the ship's
crew went ashore and quickly gathered enough wood to last
until their arrival at Fort Benton. Bidding farewell to Cody
and his party, the ship cast off and pulled into the current
once again, and began to claw its way upstream on the final
leg of the memorable voyage. The next time the riverboat
stopped would be to tie up at the wharf at Fort Benton! Will
remembered what Captain Coulson had said to him before
they left Sioux City, "Fort Benton is the end of the line. If

you want to go on from there, you'll have to go by wagon, by horseback, or on foot.''

Will knew how lucky he had been to secure passage up the river, and wondered if he would be able to match that feat as he made his way deep into the heart of Montana. He wasn't entirely sure where he was going, but he knew Fort Benton was not his final destination. Back in Sioux City he had learned that the Methodist General Conference had authorized the formation of a Rocky Mountain Conference, and that there was a church and resident pastor in Helena, so he supposed that would be his destination in Montana, more or less. The inner voice of conviction that had called him out to the line of the mountains had not named a specific place for him to go once he got there. This bit of uncertainty bothered Will not at all. He knew he was coming to where God wanted him to be, and that in His good time, the rest of the facts would be shown him. To him, all of life was a matter of walking by faith. He knew that you can almost never see the outcome at the outset, but you still have to be courageous enough to step forward and go by the light you have, until you get more light. After he got to Fort Benton he would discover how the next leg of his journey would take place, and where it would lead.

Chapter Two
...

Will awoke from his short nap much refreshed. Now that the destination had been reached, he had been able to more fully relax. He thought, too, that the sweet, fresh air of that cool summer Sunday must have had something to do with the quality of rest he had gotten. His eyes took in each detail of the room that had been his home for the better part of three weeks, and he felt a momentary twinge of sadness to be leaving the *Far West* and its captain and crew. He had come to know each one of them, and in several instances strong friendships had formed. It was indeed possible, he had learned, for a man to have a relationship with a riverboat. It was an inanimate object, he realized, but she seemed to have a personality and a style all her own, and he was fond of her. She had carried him to some of the greatest adventures of his young life, and while he was happy finally to be in Montana and ready to begin his venture there, he was not happy about leaving those good people or the good ship.

How long had he slept? A glance at his pocket watch indicated it was twenty minutes to two. He had slept a little longer than he had planned, but not dangerously so. He would still have enough time to get himself and his mind organized for the upcoming church service. He was glad, though, that he had taken the time before his nap to get the basic plan in his mind and write some notes about it. Rubbing the sleep from his eyes with thick fingers and stretching his arms, well muscled from his years on the farm and made still more sinewy from all the cutting and hauling of wood during the voyage, he wondered for just a moment if all of this were just a dream—the riverboat trip, his arrival in Montana and all that had taken place.

It took only a glance at his still-muddy boots, standing by the door of his cabin, to assure him of the reality of it all. You can't dream up gumbo on your boots and pants legs. He really was here, no doubt about it. Standing up to look out the window, he noted that the rain had not resumed and the sun was trying to peek though some holes in the cloud cover. The ground still glistened with wetness, and he supposed the gumbo was about as sticky now as it had been during his early morning walk in the rain. In many parts of the country most evidence of rain is gone a few hours after the moisture has stopped falling. In Montana, he would learn, certain places may remain wet and muddy, and puddles may still stand several days after the rain has passed.

To make himself more presentable for the worship service, he worked for a time trying to brush the worst of the mud off his boots and trousers. That on his trousers was quite dry and came off with little effort. His boots offered a greater challenge, but with persistent scraping, he got them fairly clean. At least they would be in no worse shape than everyone else's boots. Stepping out of his cabin, he discovered the boat to be deserted. Most of the crew, if not every last one of them, he knew, would be over at the Four Deuces Saloon, enjoying a hard-earned holiday after their arduous journey up the river. Soon, they would be back aboard the vessel on the downstream run. The return portion of their round trip would be with the current, of course, and so it would be faster and easier, and would require less fuel. It might also be more hazardous, particularly if their cargo happened to include a shipment of gold dust, as was often the case.

By now it was nearing 2:30, so he decided it was time to head for the Powers building where he would hold services at 3:00. The preacher, after all, should not be among the last to arrive! When he reached the makeshift church, he was at once astonished and gratified to see that the place was already half-filled with people, standing here and there in conversation groups. Most of them, he surmised, were acquainted with one another, although they were a motley collection of people. The hall had more standing than sitting room, anyway. There were no chairs, just a few rough benches. People kept coming as time for the service drew nearer, and before three o'clock the place was filled to capacity. Will was thrilled about this, and he was astounded to make the observation that in this congregation there was not a single female.

The congregation included soldiers from the fort, crewmen from the *Far West* and the *Nellie Peck*, cowboys, freight wagon drivers, local businessmen and ranchers, and some whose professions were not readily identifiable. Perhaps there were gunmen, gamblers and thieves present! No matter, each one had need to hear the word of God without prejudice.

He opened the service informally, introducing himself and telling just a little bit about who he was and where he was going. We don't know exactly how, where and when Will got the nickname that would be his for life, and would become legendary. Some say that it happened at this first service in Montana. He introduced himself as William Wesley Van Orsdel, and someone in the congregation said, "That's a pretty long handle. We'll just call you Brother Van." And so he was ever after known as Brother Van.

So honored and well-known was that name that many years later someone from the East wrote him a letter and addressed it simply "Brother Van - Montana." The letter was delivered to him without delay in Great Falls. Everyone who handled the mail knew who Brother Van was, and even to this day there are people who know the name of Brother Van who wouldn't know of whom you were speaking if you used the full name of William Wesley Van Orsdel. To his family and very best friends, he continued to be called Will, but to the tens of thousands who came to know and love him as the pre-eminent pioneer minister in Montana, he was always Brother Van.

There was no piano or organ in the hall, so the singing got off to a slow start. But with Brother Van's strong voice and his obvious enthusiasm for the singing, the others began to join in more heartily. He had them sing just the first verse of some of the more common and familiar hymns, choosing those he felt certain most of them would know. Soon, the entire congregation had gotten into the spirit of the occasion and were singing with obvious enjoyment. Brother Van opened his travel-worn Bible and read a few verses from the Sermon on the Mount in the Gospel of Matthew—verses that a good many of the men present could have recited from memory, he supposed, from the days of their childhood in Sunday schools back East. As the young preacher read, many of these strong men were remembering with tenderness what they had learned at their mother's knee and in the church back home. There wasn't much out West that reminded anyone of home; church services were one of the few points of contact, and to date there had been very little available on the frontier in the way of church services.

There is always a sense of communication between a speaker and his audience, and Brother Van knew that by now the congregation was responding to him; he had caught their attention with the singing of familiar hymns, and had gained their confidence by his unassuming air. In his brief sermon, he reminded the men that their loved ones in the East hoped they would remain true to the ideals by which they had been raised. Fellows who had not thought about much else than work and whiskey for a long time began now to think about larger issues such as honesty, concern for others, and the inner peace that comes from right living. Many of them had to admit that they had not become the kind of men their parents had hoped for, and made resolves that they would begin now to align their lives more closely with the teachings of Jesus. For an hour, the service continued with songs and sermon, scriptures and prayers, and most of those present were regretful when it concluded at four.

Just before he pronounced the benediction, Brother Van reminded the congregation that he would be holding services again in this place at eight o'clock that evening. As they left, almost every man assured the preacher he would return that evening. There was something about this husky, clean-cut young fellow that rang true. By the standards of the West, he was a greenhorn, of course. It was evident from some of his remarks that he had not yet really learned the ways of the West. But it was also evident that here was no holier-than-thou kind of preacher. He was obviously open, accepting and warm-hearted. He was also sincere in his love for Christ and in his earnest desire to see everyone accept the call to discipleship with Jesus. He had a way of seeing into people's hearts and of conveying to each person his respect and appreciation. It would not take long for the word to spread to all points on the Montana frontier that "Brother Van deals square."

It was a particular delight to Will to be so warmly and sincerely welcomed. To confess, there had been some fears and trepidation lurking in his mind. In the East, he had heard, as everyone had, the legends about the wild and woolly West, where everyone was subject to such violence. Tales were told of people who would as soon shoot you as say hello, and who were as casual about taking a life as in changing their socks. He had heard of hangings, of vigilante justice, of people having their ears cut off, of scalps being taken by savages, and so on and on. Now, here he was, and he hadn't seen anything of the sort. They were as decent and friendly as could be. It was a joyous revelation, and he put all his fears aside. He felt the assurance that he would be totally safe among these people and knew that he would not be having to defend his life or his honor while he was among them.

Although he was still in the kind of condition that had marked his arrivals in Oil City and Sioux City—penniless, homeless and jobless—he now had a sense, at least, of being at home. He didn't understand how he could feel so good about it, but he did. He had nowhere to lay his head, not a penny to his name, and there wasn't anyone who had employed him, and yet things had never been better for Will Van Orsdel. God works in mysterious ways, Will thought.

Well before eight o'clock that evening, the Powers building was filled to overflowing with people. Wonder of wonders, a lady was present! Will got to meet her before the service began, and it turned out that she was Mrs. George Baker, whose husband was the proprietor of the general store where Will had gone that morning when he was searching for a place to hold services. Mr. Baker was also present for the worship service. Following the service, the Bakers invited Will to make their home his headquarters for as long as he would be in Fort Benton, and for any other times when he might be returning. Will gratefully accepted that kind and generous offer and knew that he had found staunch and lifelong friends in the Bakers of Fort Benton.

55

So enthusiastic was the response of the people to Brother Van's singing and preaching that he was persuaded to stay on and hold services again on Monday, Tuesday and Wednesday evenings. He stayed Sunday night in his small room aboard the *Far West*, and on Monday he moved his few belongings to the Bakers' house. Wednesday was the Fourth of July holiday, and the soldiers of the fort and the local residents combined to put on a day-long celebration. Always one interested in establishing and preserving traditions, Brother Van hoped it would often be possible for him to spend the Fourth of July in Fort Benton. It marked not only the day of national independence, but it was approximately the anniversary of his arrival in Montana.

In their race upriver, the *Nellie Peck* and the *Far West* had carried full cargoes of supplies, foodstuffs and hardware. Now these goods would be distributed all across the land by wagon trains. Some of the freight wagons were pulled by strings of twenty or more oxen; others were drawn by a dozen or more horses. In these "wagon trains" a series of wagons would be hitched together in much the same way that railroad cars were coupled to make up a train. Throughout the week, as the cargoes were being unloaded and prepared for shipment, Brother Van made daily trips to talk to people, to observe the activities at the waterfront, and to inquire if part of the cargo was bound toward Helena. He rather easily found a freight wagon train that was headed for Sun River Crossing, which was some 60 miles to the southwest. It was, at least, in the general direction of Helena, and from there, he was assured, he would have no trouble catching a ride to Helena. The military garrison at Fort Shaw, just next door to Sun River, meant that there was quite a lot of travel between that place and Helena, which was one of the major cities of territorial Montana. By eastern standards, it wouldn't have been a city at all. It had come into being a few years earlier when gold was discovered at Last Chance Gulch, and was a fairly typical, rough-and-tumble mining town, but it was one of the largest settlements in Montana.

The man driving the freight wagon was glad to have company for the trip, especially that of the young preacher who was the talk of Fort Benton. On his part, Brother Van needed the ride not so much for the saving of shoe leather as for the fact that a tiny settlement on a vast prairie didn't present much of a target for a wandering stranger. By now he understood that the country was so large and so devoid of human habitation that a person taking a wrong turn could be lost for days or even weeks and could surely perish as a result.

Fort Benton sat beside the river at the bottom of a deep and wide valley, while the general lay of the land, on a plateau several hundred feet higher, was relatively level. It was a considerable strain for the horses pulling the heavily-loaded wagon to make it to the top. The trail was still muddy from the rain that had fallen in recent days, but the driver pronounced it passable. Sitting on the high seat beside the driver, Will was fascinated for a time watching the inches-thick layers of gumbo cling to the steel rims of the wagon wheel, fall off of its own weight, and be immediately replaced by a new wad of the sticky stuff.

Not many things had happened in Will's life these recent weeks that could be considered routine or uneventful, and the free ride to Sun River Crossing was no exception. Everything he did these days was a first—a new experience, either fearsome or exciting or both. This time, he was to get his first real taste of man alone against the weather on the Montana plains.

Friday, the first day's trek away from Fort Benton, passed by serenely enough. The deep and sticky mud gave them a couple of exciting moments as they made their way through some low places, but the wagon never got stuck. That night Will and the driver spread their blankets under the stars beside a cheery campfire. For a long time after the driver had fallen asleep, Will lay there, looking up at the vast expanse of cloudless, star-studded sky, and thought he had never seen anything quite so magnificent. A sense of personal well-being and of communion with God filled him, and he dropped off to a peaceful slumber.

Saturday evening, things were very different. Sun River Crossing was only a few hours distant as night was falling, and the two men agreed it would be a good idea to just keep going, arrive at the town, and be able to sleep in a good bed that night, instead of on the ground. Then, seemingly out of nowhere, a severe thunder and lightning storm broke all around them, and rain fell in torrents. In less than a minute they were totally drenched, and their teeth were chattering with the cold. In Montana, he had just learned, rain is always cold, even in the midst of summer. There was nothing they could do but keep going and hope for the best. In about half an hour, when they were both as thoroughly soaked as it was possible to get, they made out the shadowy outline of a building and drove up to it. Brother Van jumped off the wagon, ran to the door, and began to pound furiously on it. No response came from within, so he tried the door and found it unlocked. There was some dry wood in a box beside a nondescript stove, and the driver, who had the good sense to carry a weatherproof container for matches, quickly built a fire. By the light of the fire, they could see that the cabin was not currently inhabited. It was much the worse for wear, and fell far short of being rainproof, but it seemed as grand as the finest hotel to the pair, who rubbed their hands over the stove, trying to get warm again.

That night was spent more in trying to get warm than in sleeping. Their rain-soaked bedding was of no use to them.

There were no beds in the deserted cabin, but they had enough wood to keep a fire going. After what seemed interminable hours, morning came. The rain had long since stopped, and the earth was fresh and clean as they hitched up at first light to make their way into the village of Sun River Crossing. Once again it was Sunday morning, exactly a week from the day of his arrival in Fort Benton. This Sunday his arrival was in the first town he had seen in several weeks that did not lie along the Missouri River.

Like many dozens of tiny settlements that dotted the western frontier, Sun River Crossing was a village that boasted a general store and post office, a hotel, a couple of saloons, and a handful of houses in which the local residents lived. Ranchers in the outlying areas came into town on occasion to see if they had received any mail, and to procure what supplies they needed. The general store offered nonperishable foodstuffs, a small selection of yard goods and clothing and assorted hardware items.

Like the general store, the saloon was also a western institution of great importance in a community. In addition to obtaining liquor there, an inquirer could find the person he was seeking, or be informed of his whereabouts. The bartenders and saloon patrons knew everyone in the area and everything that was going on; the saloon served as a community clearing house. Most of them held public dances every Saturday night, and most of the ranchers and cowboys from the region had the custom of going to town every Saturday night, bringing their wives or girl friends if they had such, and finding a welcome change from their hard-working, lonely existence.

After a typical Saturday night, the town was sleepy and quiet as the freight wagon on which Brother Van was riding made its entrance and came to a stop in front of the general store where most of the freight was to be unloaded. But at least one person was up, and when he spied him sitting in a rocking chair on the front porch of the hotel, Will jumped down off the wagon and hastened across the street.

"Good morning, sir," he said, "I'm a Methodist preacher by the name of William Wesley Van Orsdel, and if there is any place available, I'd like to hold a church service this morning. Do you know of any place that might be suitable?"

The man fairly jumped out of his chair at this astonishing announcement, and said, "I'm mighty glad to meet you, reverend. There's never been a preacher of any kind here before, nor any church services, so this will be a very special occasion. My name is Charles Bull, and I know my wife will be as quick as I am to offer you the use of our home. We have a pretty good-sized place just a few doors down the street there." He jerked his head to the right to indicate the direction. "I think this church service will be about the biggest thing that's happened around here in a long, long time."

As he had been at Fort Benton, Will was once again astounded at the way in which these good people accepted him and readily opened their homes to him. Back East, the people were nice enough, but they were more wary of others, particularly strangers, than people seemed to be out here on the frontier.

"That's very kind of you, Mr. Bull, but don't you think we ought to go and see if your wife agrees?"

"Yep, I suppose we should, but I know right now she'll be thrilled to do it. Let's go right now and talk to her. She's probably just finishing the breakfast dishes. You had anything to eat yet this morning, son?"

"To tell you the truth, I haven't," Will replied, "My companion and I got caught in that thunderstorm last night, and we holed up in a deserted cabin we came across. It was all we could do to keep from freezing, and everything we were carrying got soaked."

"Come on, then, let's go see Mrs. Bull about a couple of things," Charles said as he stepped down off the porch and turned toward his home.

In a minute or so they were at the door of the Bulls' home, and Mr. Bull's prediction about his wife's response proved accurate. She was ecstatic to meet the young parson and eagerly agreed that the church service must be held at their home. Seeming almost to possess prior knowledge about the conversation the two men had just had, she said, "Reverend, you just come in here and sit down at the table. There's some biscuits and ham left from our breakfast, and coffee, and I'll cook you a couple of eggs as quick as anything." While she readied the food for him, she discussed how she would rearrange the living room and open the doors to the front porch, so they would be able to accommodate a pretty good-sized group of people for church.

Will could scarcely believe the warmth and openness of these wonderful people, and the breakfast this lady prepared for him was certainly among the best he'd ever eaten. "I really don't know how to thank you folks for your kindness and hospitality," he said as he wiped his lips with the napkin Mrs. Bull had provided. "The breakfast was just perfect, Mrs. Bull. I hope it's not going to be a lot of trouble for you to have the church service here." She assured him it was her pleasure to be hostess, and would be no trouble at all.

The arrival of the freight wagon had brought the town to life, and by now there were a number of people gathered around the front of the general store, hoping to see what the wagon contained. When Will had finished eating, he and Mr. Bull went back to the store. Will began to introduce himself to all those present, and both he and Charles told everyone about the church service that would be held at eleven o'clock that morning at the Bull residence.

Mr. Bull had been correct also in his estimate of how this kind of news would strike people. The arrival of a preacher at Sun River Crossing was far bigger news than the arrival of the freight wagon. Since no religious services had ever been held in that community before, it had been a very long time since any of them had gone to church. Many of those who came to settle the West had been dedicated church people in their homes in the East, and they had truly missed having the church be a part of their lives. When they said, "I'm happy to meet you, reverend," they sincerely meant they were happy.

It seemed miraculous that in the space of three hours the news of the forthcoming church service had spread not only throughout the little town, but to all of the ranches that were within several miles of town. By eleven, practically everyone in the town and outlying areas was at the Bulls' home, dressed in their Sunday best, which they hadn't had the occasion to wear recently, and ready for the service to begin.

Following the practice that had worked so well at Fort Benton, Brother Van neatly interspersed sermonizing, scriptures, songs and prayers. He was a great singer, but not a particularly great preacher. He was, however, great in his sincerity as he pled with people to make their lives follow closely in the footsteps of Jesus. He was deeply emotional, and often tears would come to his eyes as he implored people's repentance. Perhaps one of his greatest qualities was that he truly loved and appreciated people, and he was always able to treat them with kindness, courtesy and respect. People sensed his acceptance of them, and they in return accepted him. Each church service that he led became a love feast, and left everyone feeling warmly toward him and toward themselves. They found with him a sense of peace and joy which had not routinely been a part of their rugged and precarious existence on the frontier.

Will's first acquaintance with another delightful western custom came at the end of the church service, when Mrs. Bull asked if she might make an announcement. She said, "Everyone is invited to stay for dinner. Many of you ladies have brought some food, and there's plenty for all, so please stay. It will give us all a chance to get better acquainted with Brother Van Orsdel, and we hope he will return here often. By the way, reverend, would it be all right with you if we just called you Brother Van? You do seem to us to be like a brother, and to call you Brother Van just seems so natural and easy."

Will smiled at Mrs. Bull and nodded his approval. He felt very comfortable with the name, or nickname, whichever it was. It seemed as natural and easy to him as it did to the people. Brother Van it would be. It made him feel as though he really belonged.

In a short while, a great feast was ready, and after Brother Van said grace, everyone ate. Will admitted to himself and to all those sitting around him that these Montana women were wonderful cooks. He had never eaten better food anywhere. After the meal, there was a long, restful period of conversation and good fellowship. Nobody was in a hurry to leave.

But Brother Van was never content to rest for long. In the course of the after-dinner conversation he had talked with the person next to him about the contingent of soldiers stationed at Fort Shaw, just four miles to the south of Sun River Crossing. The soldiers, he was told, had been sent to protect the settlers from the Indians, some of whom were quite hostile to the whites. A majority of the white Montana settlers killed by Indians had lived within a 50 mile radius of Fort Shaw.

Mr. Bull loaned Will a saddle horse, and, accompanied by

two of his new friends, he rode to Fort Shaw around three that afternoon, and an impromptu church service was held for the soldiers. They were no less delighted to see him than the folks at Sun River Crossing had been, and they asked him to stop there at any opportunity he might have, to hold services again. Returning to Sun River Crossing, they found that a good many of the dinner guests were still at the Bulls' home, so he gathered them around for an evening vesper service before they departed to their homes.

In all the places he went in his ministry, Brother Van established friendships which would become lifelong. People responded to his warmth and sincerity in unusual ways. Asking nothing, all that he needed came to him. A saddle horse, a large white steed named Jonathan, was given to him that first Sunday by one of his new-found Sun River Crossing friends. Brother Van and Jonathan became affectionately known as "the gospel team," and the horse served him well for a number of years, until travel by train became reliable and convenient. Will had great affection for the horse, and the two of them had many great adventures.

The Bulls insisted that the visiting preacher must be their house guest, so Will stayed there Sunday and Monday nights, and spent most of Monday visiting with everyone he could meet around the town. On Tuesday, Hi Upham and Billy Phillips, two of his recently-acquired friends, rode with him north to the Piegan and Blackfeet Indian agency, near the present town of Choteau. He made some acquaintances there which led to his first opportunity, a few months later, to minister to the Indians and to participate in a buffalo hunt with them, of which more will be said later.

Hi, Billy and Will rode back from the Indian agency to Sun River Crossing, and Will stayed with the Bulls another night. The next morning he announced it was time for him to be moving on to Helena, where he hoped to get himself more

*Helena, Montana Territory, in 1865. The point from which
Brother Van's Montana ministry officially began.*

officially connected with Montana Methodism as a minister.
He knew there was supposed to be a Methodist Church
there, at least, and he hoped he would be able to meet
someone who could help him to get started. It was Saturday
evening when he rode into Helena on Jonathan, and it
appeared to him that about ninety percent of the town's
population must be in the saloons that lined both sides of the
main street. All of them were obviously doing a thriving
business that evening.

Helena, in 1872, was still in its infancy. It had a large
complement of gold-seekers, and a much larger complement
of those who had come seeking the gold-seekers. It was a
typical frontier town and mining camp, presenting both a
great challenge and great opportunity to the church. At the
first saloon that had a vacant space at its hitching rail, Will
brought Jonathan to a stop, dismounted and went inside. He

went directly up to the bar, and when the bartender came to ask what he wished to order, Will said, "I was wondering if you could tell me how to get to the Methodist parsonage. I heard there was a Methodist Church here. I'm a Methodist preacher myself. My name is William Van Orsdel, but people always call me Brother Van."

"I'm real pleased to meet, you, reverend. You heard right. The Methodist parsonage is up on the hill just to the east of here about a spit and a holler. Down that way just a bit, take a turn to your left. Right up the hill in front of you, you'll see the church, and the parsonage sits right beside it."

Thanking the man for the clear directions, Will went back out into the mid-July evening, cool but pleasant in this high mountain country. He climbed aboard Jonathan, and in a matter of minutes was at the building he correctly assumed would have to be the Methodist parsonage. A tall middle-aged man responded to Will's knock at the door. Will asked him if he was the local Methodist preacher, and when he got an affirmative response, he introduced himself.

Will learned that the minister was named J. A. Van Anda. In addition to being the pastor at Helena, he was also the presiding elder of the Helena District of the Methodist Church. The district included the entire Montana Territory, in which there was just one established Methodist church. There were 95 known Methodist members in the whole territory, and 5 Sunday schools were in operation with a total membership of 275 scholars. There was one parsonage, the one in which they were seated, which was rated as being "half-built."

Van Anda confirmed what Will had been told at Sun River Crossing and Fort Shaw: the services he had held there were certainly the first Protestant services ever held there, and quite probably the first services of any type. The words he had heard Chaplain McCabe speak in Chicago kept coming back to him, many times every day. There were, indeed, "no other foundations" out here. And it was now becoming clear to him that he was in the unique position of being able to build the church in Montana from the ground up. Every step he took as a Methodist minister was into territory where no one had ever gone before.

The Reverend Van Anda insisted that Brother Van stay the night at the parsonage. "Tomorrow morning at church," he said, "we are in for a special treat. There's a Southern Methodist bishop in town, staying with some friends from Georgia or somewhere like that, and he's going to be the guest preacher. If you would, Brother Van Orsdel, I'd like to ask you to preach at the Sunday evening service. Would you?"

Will agreed instantly, of course. On Sunday morning, a magnificent gospel sermon was preached by Bishop Marvin. Will and a good many others were stirred by the message. In the evening, hearts were stirred once again. Brother Van sang in a way that was a strong testimony in itself. He sang well, but he would not have had a career at the opera if he hadn't been a minister. Some said he made up in enthusiasm what he lacked in skill. But, his voice was pleasing, and it was certainly strong, and he used it unstintingly for the glory of God. He sang to tell a story and to put across a point. That Sunday evening in Helena, he sang one of the songs that was to become a trademark, "Diamonds in the Rough."

Will liked the song because it was a true story of the redemption of the composer, C. W. Byron. Byron had been traveling with a carnival company; in that day as in this, they were a tawdry lot for the most part. The story of Byron's conversion is told in the verses of the song:

While walking out one evening, not knowing where to
    go,
And just to pass the lone hours before we held the
    show,
The Bethel Mission Band passed, all singing with their
    might,
I gave my heart to Jesus, and left the show that night.

Chorus:
The day will soon be over, when digging will be done,
And no more gems be gathered, so let us all press on;
When Jesus comes to claim us, and says, "It is enough,"
The diamonds will be shining, no longer in the rough.

I used to dance the polka, the schottische and the waltz;
I used to love the theater, its glitter vain and false;
And Jesus, when he found me, he found me very tough,
But, praise the Lord, he saved me, I'm a diamond in the
    rough.

Chorus

One day, my precious comrades, you too were here in
    sin,
When someone sought your rescue and Jesus took you
    in;
When you are tried and tempted by sinners' stern rebuff,
Don't turn away in anger, they're diamonds in the
    rough.

Chorus

While reading through the Bible, some wondrous sights I
    see;
I read of Peter, James and John by the Sea of Galilee;

And when the Saviour called them, their work was rude
 enough,
Yet they were precious diamonds he gathered in the
 rough.

Chorus

Now keep your lamps all burning, the lamps of holy
 love,
And unto every sinner point out the way above;
The dying love of Jesus will help you love the tough;
He'll polish into beauty the diamond from the rough.

Chorus

Brother Van used this "sermon in song" effectively for
many years in many places. After a time, it became such a
tradition that he was requested to sing it almost everywhere
he went.

After the Sunday evening service, Will and the presiding
elder sat up until quite late, discussing what Will's role should
be in the newly-developing Methodist Church in Montana.
The only thing Mr. Van Anda had was Will's word as to who
he was and what his intentions were concerning his ministry.
Out West, people generally took a person at his word. If later
events proved his words untrue, it would be dealt with. But
Van Anda felt certain that this young preacher from Pennsylvania was just as eager and earnest as he purported to be,
and he felt no hesitancy at all in making him a member of
the tiny Methodist team in Montana.

Van Anda suggested that for the first year, it would be best
for Will to just work the whole Montana Territory as a kind
of missionary at large, going wherever he pleased, and
making use of whatever opportunities presented themselves.
He would be able to say that he had been appointed to this

type of ministry by the Methodist Church and was under the general supervision of Presiding Elder Van Anda.

At the next meeting of the Rocky Mountain Conference, to be held in Salt Lake City in June of 1873, Will would be up for official entrance into the Methodist work, and he would receive a regular appointment by a Methodist bishop. Until then, he had the liberty to work as a kind of "ambassador without portfolio," to help in the Methodist work as he was able, and to fulfill the preacher's mission as stated by John Wesley, Methodism's founder: "to spread scriptural holiness throughout the land."

So, for that first year, he was able to go wherever the Spirit led him. Having no regular parish assignment, he also had no income. The presiding elder's generous appointment carried no stipend! No matter; the small and occasional collections when services were held were sufficient for his needs. Back in Oil City, he had turned down the offer of $800 salary a year, plus parsonage. In his first year in Montana, his total income was $75. But he had no regrets. He had never been happier in his life. He stayed at the homes of friends who wouldn't think of accepting anything in payment for his bed and board, nor for the bed and board of his horse. He just gave himself to the work and left it to the Lord to take care of W. W. Van Orsdel. And somehow He always did. Will always managed to look quite neat and clean, as difficult as that would be for a trail rider such as he. Occasionally he would meet a friend on the street who would notice the preacher's suit was looking a little worn and thin, and he would be hustled off to a clothing store, to be fitted in a new suit. Being in the position of having to rely upon the generosity of Montana frontier people was no hardship for him; they were always more than kind and generous to him, and he never suffered any great lack, despite having no salary.

Anxious to start work on his new assignment, he pointed himself southward from Helena for a trip into the western wonderland he was beginning to think of as home. Jonathan was lame at the time, so Will was making this trip by foot, hoping to catch rides on ranchers' wagons whenever he could, and he always could, if he saw one. On this occasion, travelers of any sort were far between, and he had to walk a fairly large fraction of the distance. At every farmhouse that he sighted, he stopped to pay a call, and was usually asked to stay for a meal or even to stay overnight. Moving in this way from ranch to ranch and town to town, he made many new friends and created much new interest in getting churches and Sunday schools established. Brother Van was a stranger only once in these frontier homes. On any repeat visit, he would be welcomed like a long-lost relative, and the children would come running when they saw the stocky, black-clad figure approaching. Children knew he loved them, and they were drawn to him. In the house or on the porch, he would hold them in his lap, taking different children by turns if there were too many for one lapful. He became so familiar a figure that it was said of him years later, "There wasn't a dog in all Montana that wouldn't wag his tail when he saw Brother Van coming."

He was walking toward Bozeman, a community in south central Montana about a hundred miles from Helena, when he caught a ride with a rancher headed toward his place near the mining town of Radersburg. At the entrance to the ranch, Will jumped off the wagon, thanked the rancher for the ride, and began walking in the direction the man had said would take him into Radersburg in a short while. He was hot and tired and a little travel-worn by the time he got into town, and he was surprised to note, as he approached, that there were no welcoming faces anywhere. Instead of coming out, people were going into their houses, and were peeking at

him through the curtains. He spied one fellow standing in a
doorway with a rifle cradled in his arm, and he wondered if
he really looked that bad. Will had no idea what was wrong,
but he quickly began to get the idea that he was in the
center of something sinister. It was time for him to do
something before the situation turned ugly, but he wasn't
sure what there was he could do. So he did the only thing
he really knew how to do well.

He sang. Standing along the side of the street was an
empty wagon, with no team attached to it. Will tossed his
jacket on the low sidewall, jumped into the wagon in one
smooth motion, stood upright facing the houses, and began
to sing with all his considerable lung power. He sang as
never before, because never before had so much seemed to
hinge on his ability to communicate through song. By the
time he had sung three or four of his favorites from the
Moody-Sankey collection, well-armed citizens began to
venture out of their homes and warily approach the wagon
where the stranger in black was singing as though his life
depended on it. As soon as some of them got close enough
that he could talk to them, Will stopped singing and asked to
be told what on earth was the meaning of this sort of
welcome in a Montana town.

He learned that just a few days earlier a horse thief who
also happened to be a gunman of some renown was
supposedly headed toward Radersburg, and the citizens had
begun a vigil with the intent that the outlaw's trail would
come to its end at Radersburg. The information had been
faulty, or the outlaw had altered his course, perhaps. Will
appeared at such a time and from such a direction that the
people had some reason to believe he might have been the
outlaw whose arrival they were waiting. The mistaken iden-
tification was somewhat understandable because Will did bear
some physical resemblance to the outlaw, at a very quick

glance at the "wanted" poster. But the outlaw was not noted for his singing of gospel songs.

Hearing all of this, Brother Van laughed with relief, and said, "I'm afraid I'm not your man, folks. My name is William Wesley Van Orsdel, and I'm a Methodist preacher just trying to make my way from Helena down to Bozeman. I wanted to come by your town and meet some of the people. Are there any Methodists here?" He had done just the right thing to defuse the potentially dangerous situation. Had he tried to run for cover, as he felt like doing, he most likely would have been shot, and his own trail, not the outlaw's, would have ended prematurely at Radersburg. Running would have been interpreted as an admission of guilt; singing hymns entered a new factor into the whole confrontation.

In later years, Brother Van used to startle people by saying, "I saved a man's life once, just by my singing." Of course, the listeners would ask whose life, and he would roar with laughter as he said, "Mine!"

After many weeks, the trip to Bozeman and back to Helena was completed. Will couldn't keep full count of the number of homes where he visited, but he didn't think he had missed many of the ranches along the way, and he missed none of the towns on his route. On his return, he stopped at some of the places that he had visited on the way down, and was greeted enthusiastically in every case. It didn't matter to him or to them if the family happened not to be of the Methodist persuasion. They were friends now and had a place in each other's lives.

The custom established in these earliest months of his ministry created a tradition that was to be followed throughout his career. As he made his way around the state, he stayed in the homes of his many friends instead of spending money on hotel rooms. In most of the places he went early in his career, out in the remote regions, there were no hotels, anyway. So there came to be, in a large number of Montana homes, a room known as "Brother Van's Room," since that room was always given to him when he came to visit. In some of the larger homes, the room was unoccupied except when he was there. Most homes did not have enough space to set aside a room for such occasional use, but designated the room as Brother Van's whenever he stopped to call. He was always a welcome and appreciative guest, and his visits were eagerly awaited.

Housewives outdid themselves in preparing fine meals, and they were glad for an occasion when they could make use of their best china and silverware. Children looked forward to his visits because they loved him and he loved them, but also because their mother provided even better meals than usual when Brother Van was their guest.

By the time he got back to Helena, some of the first intimations of autumn were in the air. He'd heard much about Montana winters, but had never experienced one. Everyone said that winter on the high plains can come early in the fall and stay late in the spring. While some winters are much more mild than others, everyone had stories to tell of people who had been found frozen to death just a few steps from their own front door, which they had been unable to find in a blinding, swirling blizzard. Wisely, Will decided to listen to the advice of those who had seen several Montana winters, and not venture too far when the weather appeared threatening.

Brother Van decided that since his travels would be somewhat restricted by winter, he would do some prospecting of his own in the Prickly Pear Valley just a few miles east of Helena. Among the first people he met there were the Noteware and Riggs families, both of whom were interested in starting a church for their community, even though it was only a few miles from Helena. It was agreed that they would hold "protracted meetings" (nightly services over a period of time, such as two weeks), and the Riggs family offered the use of their home for the meetings. Attendance at the services was never large, but the level of interest shown by those who came was high. Fifteen persons made a profession of faith, and before long a new church was established. More than a hundred years later, it is still in operation and a pastor is regularly appointed there.

The coming of spring was especially welcome to Brother Van, after a rather long and severe winter. As the snow melted to give way to green grass and spring flowers, he also saw melting away the restrictions winter had placed on his activities, and he was anxious to go again into the more remote regions where he felt the people wanted and needed the church. Filled with enthusiasm from the successful protracted meetings in the Prickly Pear Valley, he decided that he would now hold a series of similar, though shorter protracted meetings 50 or 60 miles to the south, in the Jefferson River country, where there was reported to be a fairly extensive population of ranchers and a few settlements.

In the latter part of June, the popular young minister received an invitation to accompany a friend to Yellowstone National Park, which had been set aside as a national park just the previous year. Not having any commitments on his calendar for the next couple of weeks, Will was free to accept. But, in typical Brother Van fashion, he made it into a working vacation. As they passed along the upper reaches of the Yellowstone River near the park, he persuaded his friend to stop at nearly every ranch home they came to, and at one family's home he made arrangements to return on Sunday and hold church services. Going into the park, they saw the sights which park visitors in huge numbers still come to see: Old Faithful, Mammoth Hot Springs, Norris Geyser Basin, the Yellowstone River Canyon and Falls, and the many other natural wonders the park affords. He spent the Fourth of July in the park, more than 300 miles south of the place he had been a year ago, on his first Fourth of July in Montana.

Their touring of the park was delightful in every way, but the time quickly came when they had to begin the homeward journey and keep the appointment that had been made for Sunday services. Word of the impending church service had spread like wildfire throughout the region. One man observed, "If a band of buffalo ran wild through the streets of St. Louis, it would not create a bit more excitement than the news that a preacher had come to the Yellowstone."

A sizeable congregation had gathered on Sunday morning when the minister and his friend arrived. Since the house was not large enough to hold everyone, and the day was warm and fair, Brother Van stood on the doorstep to preach, while the people stood or sat in the yard, close enough to hear him easily. Like people everywhere else, these folks enjoyed the singing, and they responded warmly to Brother Van's open, friendly manner. By the time the service was over, they all felt they knew him. Here again, the hostess announced that everyone would stay for a "pitch-in" dinner—those who came had also brought food with them—and there was a wonderful meal for all, and a couple of hours of relaxed and happy visiting and conversation afterward.

It would be quite impossible to say who enjoyed these occasions more: the people or Brother Van.

Chapter Three

...

By the summer of 1873, Will already had more than ten years of experience in preaching, but it had all been on his own, on a free-lance basis. Now, officially under the supervision of the Methodist denomination, he was starting at the beginning and would go through all the necessary steps to join the Methodist ministry. Fittingly for a neophyte, his first appointment by the denomination was that of junior preacher on the Bannack-Virginia City charge, with the Reverend Francis Asbury Riggin as the preacher in charge.

Both men were born the same year, 1848, and not a great distance apart: Riggin at Baltimore, Van Orsdel at Gettysburg. Both were 25 years old when they were brought together as strangers to work as co-pastors of the Virginia City circuit. Most of the time, Riggin wore a beard, while Will never did. Riggin had lots of dark, wavy hair, while Will's was light-colored, and he was already, at the age of 25, beginning to be concerned about his receding hairline. Both men were around medium height and a bit stocky. Both could be recognized at a distance by the typical preacher's garb—wide-brimmed hat and black suit—that they always wore.

Riggin was a scholar, having earned both a bachelor's and

master's degree. So precocious was he that he entered
Baltimore City College at the age of 14 and established a
fine record as a student despite being at least 4 or 5 years
younger than the other students in his classes. By contrast,
Will had nothing more than the equivalent of a high school
education. He was intelligent, well-read and interesting, but
we have no record that he ever desired greatly to attend
college. His involvement in evangelistic work took
precedence over everything else; his desire to get out West
and serve there as a preacher was all-consuming at that time
in his life when he might have gone to college.

Riggin and Van Orsdel, in fact, made a great team. Each
one made up for what the other may have lacked. Riggin
had the rhetoric; Van Orsdel had the fire. Riggin did the
preaching, and Brother Van did the exhorting and led the
singing. Riggin was the brains and Van Orsdel was the heart
of their operation. It had been a pure stroke of genius for
the Presiding Elder to pair them up. Riggin was the more
studious; Van Orsdel was more garrulous, a hail-fellow type
of person, whose religion was highly charged with emotion.

Brother Van was not a great preacher; he was always
more of an exhorter and evangelist. His fervent plea of
"Come to Jesus!" was heard in nearly every service, and
many hundreds of people responded by committing
themselves to Christ. The strength of his presentations was
in his earnestness. He always meant what he said, and
personally practiced what he preached. As he preached, his
enthusiasm grew, as did the volume of his voice. He would
stretch forth his arms in a gesture of appeal until his stiffly-
starched shirt cuffs would pop out of his coat sleeves, and
then he would bring his arms down with a rush, slapping
his knees with his hands for emphasis. His clear, pinkish
complexion became ruddy with the energy he expended in
his preaching. He strode from one edge of the platform to

the other, not bound to the pulpit by the need to use notes.

Frequently he would reach behind his long coat-tails to bring forth a large white handkerchief, which he used to wipe the sweat from his brow or the tears from his cheeks, or perhaps to unceremoniously blow his nose. Sometimes, in the midst of a great enthusiasm for a theme he was developing, he would stop speaking and break into song, if one came to his mind which seemed to address in a special way the point he was making. His sermons were never long, but those who were present commonly went away with the feeling they had heard a message from heaven.

In the technical sense, Riggin was by far the better preacher of the two. The persuasiveness of his sermons lay in their orderly arrangement and concise presentation. His study and formal training were obvious as one heard him speak. He used his learning not as a badge of superiority, but as a sharp tool, the better to do his work. Francis Riggin was a dedicated, effective and tireless worker, but he did not have the flash of Brother Van.

Because Brother Riggin was so much more able a preacher and so much better-qualified, Brother Van was reluctant to preach in Riggin's presence very often. Rather than presenting a problem, this presented them a wonderful solution when they conducted services or held protracted meetings together. Brother Riggin did the preaching, and Brother Van did the exhorting, or "rousements," at the close of the service, imploring the sinners to repent. Riggin would reach them with his sound and logical sermons, and Brother Van, with tears in his eyes, would plead for them to "Come to Jesus." And they came.

A good part of the time, in order to cover the many preaching points on their huge parish, they went singly in separate directions. Their relationship was smooth and pleasant. They trusted and respected one another completely, and worked together most effectively and harmoniously.

Riggin, along with the Presiding Elder Van Anda, Dr. Thomas C. Iliff, and the Reverend Hugh Duncan, had just returned to Sheridan by stagecoach from the yearly meeting (called the Annual Conference) of the newly-formed Rocky Mountain Conference in Salt Lake City. Riggin commented: "Just think of it. All of the Methodist ministers of Montana riding in one stagecoach!" It was at that conference that the appointment of Van Orsdel and Riggin to the Bannack-Virginia City charge had been announced by the presiding bishop.

It was more than enough to stagger the mind of anyone from the East to consider the size of the parish to which the two young men had been assigned. Practically an empire in itself, it was larger by half than the state of Massachusetts. One of the points included in their pastoral responsibility was Salmon City, in the Idaho Territory, a good 170 miles west of Virginia City. In all that vast domain, stretching at least 200 miles from east to west, and more than 60 miles from north to south, there were known to be 18 members of the Methodist Church—one Methodist for every 666 square miles!

It was not only a monstrous-sized parish, but an important one, having within it the territorial capital, Virginia City. Forty miles north of Virginia City was the town of Sheridan, one of the major points on the charge, and it was here the two young co-pastors first met.

It was a Saturday, and that day they had the sad duty of conducting their first official service together—a funeral for Charlie Bateman, the fifteen-year-old son of a rancher, who had been killed in a farm accident. On Sunday, since the ministers returning from the Salt Lake City conference had stayed over at Sheridan, Will had the great pleasure of hearing Dr. Thomas C. Iliff (pronounced **eye**-liff) preach. Iliff was destined for future greatness in his own right, as he was

Left to right: Brother Van, Thomas C. Iliff, and Francis A. Riggin, when they were half of all the Methodist ministers in Montana.

also destined to become one of Brother Van's dearest friends. Iliff was about the same age as Will, and built exactly like him. Later, the pair would become widely known as "the heavenly twins."

Sunday afternoon, Presiding Elder Van Anda held the church's quarterly meeting with the ministers, members and officers of the Sheridan congregation. Giving the two young preachers some helpful advice and instructions as to how they might manage their heavy responsibilities, he departed for Helena the next morning. The two dauntless young pioneers were on their own now to build the Kingdom within their giant parish. With only one member for every 666 square miles, they were certainly beginning from scratch. Lesser men than they might have shrunk from such a challenge, believing the task to be more than was humanly possible. Such a thought seems never to have entered the mind of either one of them.

As soon as they were left alone, the two pastors sat down to talk things over. Good Methodists, they agreed at once that they had to have a plan by which to accomplish something of significance. One big problem was how they could conduct Sunday services in as many places as possible, as regularly as possible. With the limitations of travel by horseback, even if they went singly in different directions, the best they could do would be to offer Sunday services to each settlement about once every 6 weeks, with perhaps another worship service on a weekday evening each 6 weeks or so. They hoped a better solution would present itself.

Riggin agreed with his junior partner that in order to create greater interest and to build church membership, it would be important to hold a series of protracted meetings in every community, settlement, or country school in their parish. It was a most ambitious undertaking, but they couldn't think of a better way to meet their people and learn their way around their parish. The solution for which they prayed finally came to them. They decided that only one of them would accept definite preaching appointments for each Sunday or special observance. They would start out together, and in places where it seemed a revival would be workable, they would stay. The preacher with the next engagement would leave when he had to, and the other would remain to finish up the series of meetings. Since they could not be in all places at all times, their plan seemed the most workable alternative. At least it would permit them to systematically cultivate their parish.

It was their aim to establish churches at each of the preaching points in their parish, and to do this required a group of committed Christians who would carry on some church activities in the ministers' absence, maintaining a Sunday school in particular. The people who lived in the communities, even if they remained uninvolved in church matters, were very much in favor of seeing a church established. It would give stability to the community and be a continuing influence for good. Brothers Van and Riggin were very likable, personable young men, and people were naturally drawn to them. They were also drawn to the idea of making their home place into a "real" community by having a church there.

The people on the frontier needed religion, and many of them were aware of it. Life was difficult and tenuous; death and grief were all too common. To have the resource of Christian faith at one's disposal could be the thing that would make life bearable and give them the courage to carry on. What Brother Van and Riggin were offering was hope, and it struck a responsive note in the settlers.

The obvious first step in creating a church was to hold revival meetings and get some converts who would be the nucleus. In a good many cases, the people living in the communities had been good church members before they came out west, and needed only the opportunity to become re-committed to Christ and the church in their new home.

In October the two ministers began a series of meetings at Fish Creek, near the present town of Whitehall. For three weeks the services continued with great public interest and the net result was that 30 persons joined the church. This was the most far-reaching revival that had ever been held in Montana up to that time, and Brother Van wrote of it, "Any persons who were skeptical about the 'old-time religion' had their minds disabused by the singing, praying and shouting at these meetings."

Brother and Sister Jordan were among the most prominent persons of the Fish Creek community, as well as the most active participants in the lengthy revival. They insisted that Brothers Van and Riggin make their home their headquarters during the meetings. Mrs. Jordan's mother, Grandma Tuttle, lived with them, as did their lovely daughter Ida. We have no reason to think that Will had any romantic notions about Ida, but having a lovely young lady present at the meetings and in the home where they stayed obviously added considerable interest to things in general. Certainly it did for Mr. Riggin, because not many months later, Ida Jordan became Mrs. Riggin.

November saw the youthful team 12 miles north of Virginia City, opening a series of meetings at the Taylor School in the Ruby Valley. Two weeks of services there netted them 14 new church members. Then, moving about a day's ride further north, they held forth for three weeks in the town of Sheridan. There, 25 souls were added to the growing church membership. Under the good leadership of Brother Hugh Duncan, their predecessor, a new church building had been begun, and it was now completed. Around the first of December, when the presiding elder came through, the formal dedication services were held. Sheridan could then boast of being the fourth Methodist Church in Montana, the other three being located at Helena, Bozeman and Virginia City.

Starting off the new year in true form, on January first, 1874, Riggin and Brother Van began a series of meetings at Bannack. Until 1865, Bannack had been the territorial capital, and an important gold-mining town. The Bannack crusade resulted in 14 new members being added to the growing Methodist parish family.

All told, the evangelistic crusade on their parish from September through February resulted in a gain of 150 members, a growth of close to one thousand percent in just six months. Add to this the fact that they met the future Mrs. Riggin, and it was an astonishingly successful half-year. In each community where a revival was held, they obtained enough commitments to Christ to provide a strong core of leadership around which a new church could be formed.

In February the weather was mild enough that Brother Van and Riggin felt it would be safe to ride their horses from Sheridan to Helena to attend the first District Conference ever held in Montana. The meeting would bring together everyone involved in the Methodist ministry in Montana. Since getting there would involve a journey of several days by stagecoach or on horseback for most of them, the district meeting was slated to last for two weeks. Rather than just deal with their own internal affairs for all that time, though, the band of ministers decided to occupy their time by holding a two-week series of revival meetings in Helena. They would meet together to talk over their business matters in the mornings, do parish visiting in the afternoons, and hold the revival services in the evenings. This effort brought 35 new converts under the care of the new pastor in Helena, W. C. Shippen, and substantially strengthened the church in Helena.

On the second night of services, Brother Van taught the people one of his favorite songs, "The Gospel Train is Coming." At that time, the railroad lines nearest Montana were 450 miles south, at Ogden, Utah. Everyone wondered how long it would be until Montana had train service. By now, railroads already existed on all sides of the territory, and in order to complete the nationwide network, trains would eventually have to come to Montana. For that reason, the song had more than the usual appeal to Montanans.

It happened that one of the worshipers that night was the man who owned and operated one of Helena's most notable "hurdy-gurdy" houses, as saloon and dance hall establishments were called. He was so taken with the singing of the "Gospel Train" song that he told Will at the close of the services, "Brother Van Orsdel, if you will promise to sing that gospel train song again tomorrow night, I will promise to personally bring 40 sinners to the services." Brother Van accepted at once, of course. And the fellow was as good as his word. The next night he was there, sitting in the front row, with well over the 40 men he had promised to bring, and a few dance hall girls added for good measure. Will sang "The Gospel Train is Coming" and several other favorites such as "Diamonds in the Rough," "Harvest Time," and "O Happy Day" just for that delegation, as promised.

The saloon-keeper was delighted with the songs, but he hadn't counted on getting religion in the process. He was surprised, at the close of the service, to find himself kneeling at the altar, his wife beside him, surrendering his heart to the Master. He sold his saloon and dance hall to enter a more respectable business, and the couple became staunch supporters of the Methodist church in Helena.

When the meetings in Helena concluded, the clergymen rode off to return to their parishes. Brothers Van and Riggin saddled their horses and pointed them south to the Beaverhead country, to hold a series of meetings near the present town of Dillon. When they arrived, they were deeply impressed to learn of the Christian dedication of Sister Jane Selway, who had developed a very good Sunday school program in the Beaverhead. For the first four years, she had worked unassisted, and for the last two years, the Reverend Hugh Duncan had been able to offer occasional assistance. No more than about ten families lived in the whole area, but Will and Riggin called in their homes by day, and got them all out for the evening services. The Beaverhead area was to become his heart's home in an important way, but at this particular time of his life, it was another one of the points on the gigantic parish he and Brother Riggin were trying to serve.

Thirteen new church members were received as the result of their evangelistic efforts in the Beaverhead. Brother Van always took the trouble to keep a record of how many people were present, how many were converted, and how much money was given in the offering, as a matter of history, but he didn't really care that deeply about the numbers. He would just as happily preach to a group of 5 persons as to 500, and he would be just as fervent, eloquent and persuasive for an offering of $1.62 as for $1600. He and Riggin felt satisfied with the response they were receiving. Given the sparse population of their parish, their accomplishments were phenomenal. Everywhere they went, enough people responded to the altar calls to provide a strong nucleus around which to build a church. And there were large numbers of people getting used to the idea of going to church services whenever Brother Van or Riggin came to their community.

Now, at last, they were ready to make a frontal assault on the Sodom of their realm, the territorial capital, Virginia City. It was to be the most intensive campaign of their year, and they had spent more than six months getting their evangelistic techniques fine-tuned. Now they were ready for this major challenge.

Nevada's Virginia City was a lusty silver-mining settlement, but it was tame as a kitten compared to the Virginia City in the Montana Territory. Road agents (bandits) did a thriving business holding up stagecoaches and were considered by most people to be a more dangerous threat than the hostile Indians who also inhabited the region.

Virginia City was, in fact, the second wave of the frontier development in the southwest corner of the territory of Montana. A major gold strike had been made in 1862 at Grasshopper Gulch, near Bannack, and the great rush of people to that area had been responsible for Bannack being named the first territorial capital. The cream was quickly skimmed off the Grasshopper Gulch diggings, and gold became hard to find around Bannack. When Henry Edgar and Bill Fairweather came into Bannack to buy supplies around the first of June in 1863, there were more than three hundred prospectors who were not making wages on their Grasshopper Gulch diggings.

Edgar and Fairweather, quite by accident, had found gold at Alder Gulch, the mining district which made Virginia City famous. The first pan of gravel they washed yielded $2.50 worth of gold flakes, which was roughly the equivalent of a full day's wages, or more. When they went to Bannack, they had every intention of keeping the discovery to themselves, and they didn't say a word to anyone about it. But there was an aura of excitement that surrounded them which they could not suppress, and which the gold-hungry prospectors at Bannack had been able to sense. Without a word by Edgar or Fairweather, the news nevertheless was out: GOLD DISCOVERED AT ALDER GULCH!! The three hundred prospectors followed them back to their diggings, and the rush was on.

In less than two years, Virginia City sprang into being, boasting a population of more than 10,000 persons. It was by far the largest city in the territory, so the territorial capital was moved there from Bannack in 1865. The territorial governor had his residence and office in Virginia City, but it was Satan who ruled the roost there.

Probably more than $50,000,000 worth of gold was extracted from Alder Gulch. Other large amounts came from Grasshopper Gulch, Last Chance Gulch, White's Gulch, Garnet, Gold Creek, Elkhorn, and other Montana locations literally too numerous to mention. More than 500 sites in Montana produced gold over the years, and some are still producing. It is small wonder that Montana adopted as its official nickname "The Treasure State," for it has produced mineral treasures of enormous importance, not only from the gold fields, but also the copper bonanza that gave the city of Butte the title of "the richest hill on earth."

Virginia City had all the problems that go with the gold: gambling, prostitution, alcoholism, crime and poverty. But even in the gold camps where crime and corruption were so rife, most of the people were decent, hard-working and God-fearing. The territorial governor, B. F. Potts, and a number of other high government officials were regular in attending the services which Brother Van and Riggin conducted, and they soon became close friends. It was the start of a long tradition, for Brother Van was the friend and confidant of every Montana territorial and state governor from that time forward.

To open the crusade, they invited Dr. Thomas C. Iliff, the Methodist pastor at Bozeman, to come to Virginia City and preach for eight consecutive nights. A fiery and eloquent speaker, Iliff was considered to be one of the finest preachers of that day in any denomination, and was, of course, a good personal friend of the Brothers Van and Riggin. The large hall they had engaged was filled to capacity each night. From that gospel onslaught, thirty new church members were enrolled at Virginia City, and the church was firmly established there.

The main stagecoach line serving the area came north from Ogden and Corinne, Utah to Bannack, and then went 70 or 80 miles to the northeast, to Virginia City. Gold from the south-central Montana gold fields such as Grasshopper Gulch and Alder Gulch either had to go by stage southward to Utah, from whence it could be shipped by train to the East, or by stage northward to Fort Benton, where the gold would be loaded aboard a steamship for the trip downriver to Sioux City. While locomotives and riverboats could also be robbed, and sometimes were, they were not nearly as vulnerable as the stagecoach, driving many miles across the wilderness, with only its own tiny crew to defend it against attack.

A gold shipment was considered a plum ripe for the picking by the road agents, who rallied to the harvest with such zeal that it soon became nearly impossible to get the precious metal through without their intervention. Highwaymen, it seemed, lurked behind every bush and boulder along the trail, awaiting the approach of the next stagecoach. Faces masked with bandanas, and their revolvers leveled menacingly upon the driver and passengers, the robbers would relieve the stagecoach of any of its cargo that seemed valuable, and then would often proceed to take whatever money and jewelry the passengers had.

Whether such an event really happened is open to some question, but a legend persists that upon one occasion when Brother Van was riding a stagecoach, it was held up by a masked gunman. Ordering the driver down from his perch and the passengers out of the coach, the bandit lined them up and proceeded to rob them all individually, collecting money, watches, rings, and whatever else he saw that he fancied. When he came to Brother Van, the preacher asked, "You wouldn't rob me, would you? I'm just a poor Methodist preacher." The bandit passed him by in the line, saying, "Of course I wouldn't rob you, reverend. I'm a Methodist myself!" (An alternate version of the story has the bandit saying "I'm a preacher myself.")

Road agents were mean and dangerous and were certainly not known for their politeness and consideration of others. One road agent made the boast that he would just as soon shoot a man as eat breakfast. He was not the only one so inclined. The settlers had good reason to fear and despise them.

Henry Plummer was the personable young sheriff of Bannack. Those who elected him to office did not know, of course, that when he was not busy enforcing the law in Bannack, he was busy breaking it elsewhere. In truth, Plummer was the head of a road agent band that plagued the settlers' lives.

A mountaineer who happened also to be a member of the Masonic lodge died of tick fever, and at his funeral in Virginia City he was accorded the full Masonic rites. When the band of Masons had assembled, they were surprised to see how many of them were settlers in that region. At that time, they organized a Vigilance Committee, dedicated to the eradication of outlawry in the region, with special emphasis on ridding the area of road agents. Rapidly their fame spread as under the Vigilantes' brand of raw frontier justice, one desperado after another fell victim to their hanging nooses. The circle of citizens' arrests and summary executions continued until finally the Vigilantes even captured Sheriff Plummer, and promptly hung him, on Sunday evening, January tenth, 1864.

In the space of just three months, from December 1863 until February 1864, the Vigilantes captured and executed 24 road agents. In the following year, nine more were hung. So thorough were the Vigilantes in carrying out their mission that in 1866, a shipment of gold valued at $1.5 million was freighted from Helena to Fort Benton, and then was shipped downriver to St. Louis without mishap. Just a couple of years earlier, such an undertaking would have been all but impossible. The Vigilantes had accomplished their objective of making Montana safe for the general populace. We do not support or approve the notion of people taking the law into their own hands, but it certainly worked in that instance. It may also have been truly necessary to deal with the road agent problem in such a way, considering that the law was corrupt, and not working to defend the people.

By the time March rolled around, Riggin and Brother Van had made the rounds of their Montana parish, holding a series of meetings in every community, and visiting in virtually every ranch home in their huge parish. But they had yet to make contact with the "out-point" on their charge, Salmon City, Idaho. It appeared that the real winter weather was over, and that it would be reasonably safe now for them to make the 170-mile trek through the mountains to the west. It was, of course, all unmarked country, with hardly any roads or trails for one to follow. A cowboy who was a member of their church in Virginia City said he felt comfortable about being able to find the way, so they persuaded him to lead their expedition. The two ministers and their guide set out early one March morning for Salmon City.

Apparently, in saddling his horse that morning, Pastor Riggin had been uncharacteristically careless, or perhaps he had not yet been fully awake. They had not gone far along the trail when his horse shied, jumping sideways when he was startled by a rabbit in the brush. As the horse jumped, the saddle slipped to the horse's side, depositing Riggin very unministerially upon the ground. "Say, Francis," hooted Brother Van, "It looks like your horse has lost its 'riggin'!"

The second day of their journey, they came to the foot of the mountains they would have to cross, by way of Bannock Pass. There they found a ranch house which their cowboy guide told them was in fact an inn operated by a man named Hamilton. Alighting from their horses, the three were greeted in the front yard by Mr. Hamilton, a typical old-timer and frontiersman. Riggin told him they needed supper, a place to sleep, and hay for their horses, and the man agreed to provide all three necessities. Tired from their long ride, and anxious to get to bed so as to get an early start the next day in going over the pass, the travelers didn't get around to visiting with Mr. Hamilton that night. They just fed and bedded down their horses, ate their supper, and went to bed.

Eating breakfast by lamplight early the next morning, Riggin asked their host what the charge would be for their food and lodging. Hamilton replied, "Well, I've been studying some about that, wondering who you fellows might be, and I've decided you must be either gamblers or preachers, because

nobody but those two classes wears 'biled' shirts." "Now,"
he continued, "if you are gamblers, I want the full price, two
dollars a man. But if you're preachers, I'll just take it out in
praying. I could sure use a professional psalm-singer puttin' in
a few good words for me."

Riggin assured him they were not gamblers, but were in
fact the Methodist pastors for that area. He said, "If you can
produce a Bible, we'll show you. Our own are packed in our
saddlebags, and we could go and get one if you don't have
one handy." Mr. Hamilton only had to turn around to pull
the family Bible off the shelf, and hand it to Riggin. Riggin
opened it to a passage from the Psalms he especially liked
and read a few verses in his most professional voice. Closing
the Bible, he turned to Will and said, "Now, Brother Van
Orsdel, you pray."

When the impromptu devotions were over, Hamilton had
become convinced they were bona fide preachers, and as the
trio were ready to depart, he told them, "You gentlemen
have a free lifetime pass at my place any time you happen to
be passing through. I'll take good care of you and your
horses, and you can pay your bill in prayer."

Their trip the rest of the way to Salmon City was made
without mishap. Their cowboy guide brought them through,
precisely on target. In the town they found a strong current
of interest in the establishment of a Methodist Church. In a
week of meetings, the two ministers organized a group of
people and initiated the process for getting a new church
chartered. As they were making the return trip to Virginia
City, they once again stayed the night at Mr. Hamilton's inn
and paid their bill with prayer.

Everywhere they went on the frontier, they were received
in this manner. People who lived miles from anywhere didn't
see anyone outside the family for weeks at a time, and it was
a special occasion when someone came to visit. When it was

someone as genuine, kind and decent as Brothers Van and Riggin, the hosts were always glad for them to stay as long as they could, and urged them to return as soon as possible.

Methodist ministers are required to attend the annual meeting of the conference to which they are assigned. At Annual Conference, there are reports and committee meetings, preaching services, the ordination of ministers, and the reading of the ministerial appointments for the coming year. The annual meeting of the Rocky Mountain Conference was held in August of 1874 in Salt Lake City, Utah.

Will had never attended an Annual Conference and had only seen one bishop in his life. Being in his usual penniless condition, it didn't look like he would be able to attend this one either. He was very happily surprised one day to receive in the mail a check for one hundred dollars from Governor Potts, with the friendly instruction that he was to use it to cover the expenses of attending Annual Conference. Will was elated, to say the least.

The journey would be made by stagecoach to Corinne, Utah, and from there they would go by train to Salt Lake City. After Brother Van and Riggin boarded the stagecoach at the John Selway ranch in the Beaverhead valley, it was carrying seven passengers: all six of the Methodist ministers in the Montana territory plus one representative from the national Methodist Mission Society, Dr. J. M. Reid, the first national denominational official ever to visit Montana Methodism. The Montana ministers were delighted to see one another, after working so long in their own separate domains. Between members of the clergy there is a strong and warm bond of brotherhood. To one Methodist minister, another is practically family. What was going on in that stagecoach was, sure enough, just like a family reunion.

To reach Corinne, Utah required four days and three nights of uninterrupted travel. Horses and drivers were changed at intervals, but the passengers stayed on, mile after rocky mile, day after grueling day. By now, Will had learned how to ride a stagecoach, having had some experience at it the last couple of years. At first one's tendency is to brace himself against the jolts, but he rather soon learned that this is no help, and only serves to accentuate the jostling one must take. The proper way, he found, is to just settle back in your seat, relax, and let yourself sway with the coach, instead of resisting its motions. This method, he found, eliminated much of the jarring and jolting and even permitted a certain amount of semi-restful sleep.

But sleep was not a major concern for this coach filled with Methodist preachers, who tend to be a fun-loving lot. They were having a glorious time swapping stories of their frontier adventures and humorous incidents in their churches. Whenever there was a lull in their story-telling, they would sing. Anyone desiring a unique and stirring experience should find his way to a conference of Methodist ministers and listen to the singing! Each driver who took his turn at the high seat on the stagecoach got off remarking that he had never heard or seen anything like that before in all his life.

Will had not fully appreciated how great a movement he was a small part of until he attended that conference. Ministers were present not only from Montana, but from Utah, Idaho and Wyoming as well. He heard pastoral reports much like his own from pastors he had not even known existed, serving places he had never heard of, and he was impressed at how great a movement Methodism was. Bishop Thomas Bowman presided over the conference, and Will was greatly impressed not only by the bishop's gentle and efficient way of handling the business of the conference, but also by his humble and inspired preaching.

Sunday was the final, climactic day of Annual Conference. It began, of course, with the bishop preaching and a great choir singing at the Sunday morning service. In the afternoon several of the Montanans went sightseeing around the city. While touring the great "Mormon" temple, they stayed to hear the Mormon bishop preach. That evening, at the final session of conference, there was a worship service, followed by the bishop reading the appointments. With the singing of "Blest be the Tie that Binds our Hearts in Christian Love," the conference was adjourned and the band of ministers began to dissolve, each returning to a position on the front line of service. Brother Van and Riggin were delighted to have been reappointed to the Virginia City-Bannack circuit, and the people back home were equally as delighted to have them remain.

When they returned to their parish, they found interest running so high in the Virginia City church that it would be necessary for one of the ministers to be there for church services every Sunday. At that time they also launched an effort to build a church of a suitable size, since the plain wood-frame structure they had been using had become quite inadequate for their needs. Money for the new building was donated generously, and it was not long until a fine stone building stood, ready for occupancy, on the site that had been purchased.

While the weather was still warm enough for outdoor camping, Brother Van and Riggin and some friends made a trip into Yellowstone Park. Will hoped to see all the sights he had missed the year before. One night, he and Riggin spread their blankets on the ground, and were just drifting off to sleep, when a small geyser nearby erupted unexpectedly, showering them with very hot water. Jumping up, they both grabbed for blankets and began to pull, hoping to get out of the area before more water hit them. The problem was that they had both gotten hold of the same blanket and were pulling in opposite directions. Just when they had pulled each other to a standstill, the geyser erupted in earnest, leaving both men sputtering and thoroughly drenched, as was all their bedding and extra clothing. The rest of the night was spent in an unsuccessful attempt to get warm and get their bedding and clothing dried out. Telling of the incident later, Riggin said, with a hearty laugh, "One thing is certain. That incident taught us the value of cooperation!"

They were still in the park when Sunday morning came around, and the two ministers decided they must have church services. They invited the other touring parties who were in their campground to join them in worship, and a number of them accepted the offer. Brother Van naturally got the assignment of leading them in song, and since there happened to be some good singers in the group, they sang quite a number of old and new hymns with real enjoyment. Then Brother Riggin gave a short but eloquent sermon. It was, quite certainly, the first preaching service ever held in the Lower Geyser Basin of Yellowstone National Park.

Will had not had the opportunity to take part in a Christmas program since leaving his home in Pennsylvania, so he was particularly delighted, in the Christmas season of 1874, to find the ladies of the Beaverhead Valley busily preparing a Christmas extravaganza. The children were all greatly excited about it, perhaps as much as Brother Van was. It would be at the Poindexter School, where all the community gatherings and the infrequent church services were held. In addition to the local residents, people who lived in the surrounding gold-mining camps of Bannack, Argenta and Grasshopper Gulch had been invited to the party.

An extra coach had to be put on the Beaverhead Rock Stage Line to carry all the people who responded to the invitation, and on the night of the program the school was filled to overflowing with excited children and adults.

Sister Jane Selway, the superintendent of the Sunday school, was the chief planner and promoter of the project, and for several months before Christmas, preparations for the great event had been taking place. Christmas tree decorations were not available in the local general store, so the resourceful frontier ladies and, of course, the children, had made everything that was used to trim the tree and decorate the building. The place fairly sparkled with Christmas cheer, and Will felt certain he had never seen a more beautiful Christmas tree than the Montana fir that stood in all its glittering grandeur in the corner of the school's solitary classroom.

An interesting and amusing program of skits, songs, and recitations was presented by the children, and at the close of those presentations, Santa Claus made a dramatic appearance and gifts were distributed to every man, woman and child who was present. Cocoa, sandwiches and cake were then served, and everyone stayed around as long as possible, reluctant for the magical evening to come to an end.

The occasion was memorable to Brother Van because it caused him to feel more strongly than ever his comradeship with these wonderful frontier people. They were, indeed, as big and beautiful as the land where they lived, and he counted it an honor to be one of them. He had known from the start that coming to Montana was the right choice for him to make, but the Beaverhead Christmas celebration cemented it for all time. Life here as a pioneer minister was even more wonderful than he had dreamed it would be, and he knew he was doing what he had been born to do. His heart at Christmas was full of love, joy, and peace, and there was nothing he lacked. Except, perhaps, a fine woman with whom to share it all. Brother Riggin had gotten lucky; now it was his turn.

Chapter Four

• • •

*W*hile it is true there were a good
many white settlers killed by hostile Indians in Montana,
there were only two full-scale Indian battles. One was the
Battle of the Little Big Horn, more commonly referred to as
"Custer's Last Stand" or "the Custer Massacre." The other
was the Battle of the Big Hole, and in that historic
encounter, Brother Van played a significant role.

At the Annual Conference session in the summer of 1875,
after serving two happy and eventful years with Francis
Riggin on the Virginia City-Bannack circuit, Brother Van
was assigned as preacher in charge of the Sheridan and
Bannack portion of the parish, while Riggin was assigned to
the Virginia City sector. This new arrangement vastly
reduced the size of the parish Brother Van had to cover.
His domain, 2½ times the size of Rhode Island, was now a
mere 75 miles east to west and about 40 miles north to
south, all of it to be covered by horseback.

As a roving missionary, it was his duty to visit in all the
homes, conduct services in as many places as possible as
often as possible, and perform the ministerial rites for
funerals, weddings and baptisms. Having worked in this
region for two years already, Brother Van was not only
well-acquainted with the towns and the people, but knew

the hills and valleys, rivers and stream beds better than many
who had lived there much longer.

In the months following his assignment to his new post,
Brother Van was dismayed to learn of the increase of
hostilities between the Native Americans and the white
settlers, since he had ties with and affection for both sides in
the dispute. Once again, July Fourth came into prominence in
his life, for it was then he first learned of the fate that had
befallen Custer and his men at the Little Big Horn. His thin-
ning hair practically stood on end as he heard that two of the
leaders of the Indians who had wiped out Custer's whole
contingent were Sitting Bull and Rain-in-the Face, the same
two chieftains who had stood on the deck of the *Far West*
that day in 1872 on the upper Missouri and had behaved
quite civilly toward the whites.

He was also greatly interested to learn of the important role
that "his" steamship, the *Far West*, had played in the Custer
drama. At the time he secured passage on the *Far West*, Will
couldn't have known how fortunate he was to have found
that particular vessel preparing to embark at Sioux City. It
was an admirable ship. Throughout a long and colorful
career, she continued to set new speed records, while perfor-
ming some important missions in the settlement of the west.

Exactly four years after having taken young Will Van
Orsdel up to Fort Benton, the *Far West*, in June of 1876, was
steaming up the Yellowstone River at the mouth of the
Powder River (near the present town of Terry) on the
morning of June 15 when Major General George A. Custer
began his ill-fated march toward the Little Big Horn.

Captain Grant Marsh, probably the most noted of all the
western riverboat captains, was in command of the *Far West*
at the time. The vessel had been leased to the United States
Army for $360 per day, and was being used to carry supplies
to military forces which were attempting to quell Indian

uprisings in several regions of the Montana frontier. After the departure of Custer's troops, Captain Marsh took his ship up the Yellowstone to its confluence with the Tongue River and then on upstream to the confluence of the Rosebud River, arriving at the encampment of Colonel John Gibbon on June 21. Terry and Custer, with their military contingents, met Colonel Gibbon near the point where the Big Horn River joins the Yellowstone, and on board the *Far West* the council of war took place during which plans were formulated for the Seventh Cavalry's now-famous disastrous attack upon the Indians.

At first light on June 22nd, the *Far West's* crew unloaded 15 days' worth of supplies for Custer's troops. The troops were variously engaged in their battle preparations. Some were inspecting and cleaning their equipment yet another time. Many were writing letters home, and it was apparent to the crew of the *Far West* that a feeling of gloom, perhaps of impending disaster, was hanging heavy in the air, affecting the cavalrymen as well as the ship's crew.

After Custer's troops had ridden off to the south, the *Far West* followed them, steaming up the Big Horn to the place where the Little Big Horn River joins it. The *Far West* was one of the few ships capable of maneuvering on some of these smaller, shallow tributary rivers, and the Army had done well in engaging her services. By dawn of June 27th, the *Far West* had come as far upstream as it was possible to go, to a point that turned out to be within 15 miles of the site of the battle.

About ten o'clock that morning, while the captain and his crew were speculating about what kind of battle may have occurred and what its outcome may have been, a lone rider appeared. Naked save for a loincloth, and holding his rifle aloft in a gesture of peaceful intent, the rider was finally recognized as "Curly," one of the Indian scouts of the

Seventh Cavalry. Quickly taken on board the ship, Curly broke into a violent demonstration of grief. Curly could speak only the Crow language and there was nobody on the *Far West* who could translate it, so it took nearly two hours of signing and gesturing for Curly to impart the message that Custer and all his men were dead.

During the next three days, many wounded men from various other commands were brought to the *Far West*. General Terry and some of his staff arrived, and, setting up emergency headquarters on board the ship, Terry ordered Captain Marsh to take her back to the Yellowstone and then downstream to Bismarck (Fort Abraham Lincoln) in the Dakota Territory as fast as she could possibly go. The downstream run was made at a speed never equalled by any other craft on either the Missouri or the Yellowstone in the riverboat era.

The legend persists that it was the *Far West* that first brought news to the outside world of the Custer Massacre, but like many legends, it is not true. On June 27, General Terry wrote a dispatch to General Sheridan, who was 240 miles away at Fort Ellis, and sent a cavalryman to deliver it. At Fort Ellis (near Bozeman) there was a telegraph available, so the world had heard of the Custer Massacre before the *Far West* reached Bismarck on July 5. Still, the *Far West's* daredevil race down the Yellowstone was an epic voyage. Running near the danger point on the boilers' gauges all the way, the ship was in constant jeopardy of overheating and exploding. Narrowly missing islands, shoreline, and snags in the water, the craft dashed forward at speeds up to 20 miles per hour, occasionally brushing an obstacle and sending the crew tumbling like tenpins from the impact. Once on the voyage they had to stop, to hold a hasty funeral service for a soldier who had died of wounds received in battle. They reached Fort Abraham Lincoln at eleven o'clock on the night of July 5, having traveled approximately 1000 miles in 54 hours—an amazing average speed of about 18½ miles per hour.

Will could easily understand the Indians' side in resisting the invasion of whites. He knew that in the era of westward expansion, the Indians' prior claims on lands and hunting grounds were generally ignored by the white migrants. Treaties were lightly made and just as lightly broken, each successive arrangement being good only until the whites found it more to their advantage to alter it. He also understood that to fight to protect one's land, home and family is one of the most basic human reactions.

Already it was becoming obvious that the reservations promised to the Indians were generally located in areas thought to be of no possible value or use to the whites.

The United States, in acquiring the Louisiana Territory from France in 1803, acquired also the right to explore, and go in and possess, that vast new area, of which Montana was a part. But Brother Van knew that we did not, in that $15 million transaction, buy the many tens of thousands of Indians who had lived there for untold generations. Above all, Indians were people, and it seemed to Will that his government often lost sight of that.

One of the fine tribes of Indians in the West were the Nez Perce, who made their home in the Wallowa Valley in eastern Idaho. Joseph, the Nez Perce chief, resisted when the government began to pressure him to take his people and leave their ancestral home in the Wallowa Valley, to allow the white settlers to come in and take over. The Nez Perce had been assured by the government they would be allowed to keep their home country.

Chief Joseph was a remarkable man, as decent and courageous as he was intelligent. Joseph was a young boy when a missionary named Spalding came to the Wallowa

Valley to work among the Nez Perce. Joseph, when he was an old man, said of him, "Spalding show Injun how plow ground, raise wheat, raise heap thing. Spalding teach Injun read, write, make map. Me and my brother go to school. Spalding know I chief someday; he heap teach me. Spalding tell Injun about Jesus hang on cross. Spalding say Injun all same white man brother. Injun believe Spalding.

"My people always good to white man. You know Nez Perce never raise tomahawk and hit white man before my war in eighteen seven-seven. One day, two year before war come, white men kill one Injun. My people heap mad. They want kill one white man. I say no."

There were several occasions when Joseph denied the pleas of his braves to fight. Some thought this meant he was afraid, and they gave him the nickname "old woman." This derision was too much for Chief Joseph, so he did finally take the warpath against the whites, who had literally been asking for it for years.

Brother Van's parish in southwestern Montana was not very far removed, geographically, from the Wallowa Valley. News seeping into the mining camps of Bannack, Argenta and other places caused a certain amount of local alarm. Reports grew more numerous of raids by Indians on ranches of white settlers, with people being killed, livestock stolen, and buildings burned. Soon it became apparent that the Nez Perce had forsaken their peaceful ways and a state of war existed.

While Brother Van felt the Indians had good reason to be outraged, he could not help joining forces with the white settlers, for they were his parishioners. He knew them; he stayed in their homes. He married and buried and baptized them. He was their minister and they were his people. Their homes and ranches, and even the businesses in towns, were now at stake, as well as their very lives.

As stories of Indian atrocities were told, the settlers knew it was time for them to dig in and prepare to defend their homes and their lives. Will later wrote of those days, "The miners and ranchmen were so engrossed by the coming war that they did not need the services of a sky pilot and would not come out to hear me preach." It was not a blow to Will's ego. He understood perfectly why a family would not undertake a trip across the prairies and hills, exposing themselves to attack, if it could be avoided. He wouldn't want anyone to die because they were going to church.

A state of siege existed, and while he was thus forcibly unemployed, Brother Van decided he should do something to make himself useful if he could. General O. O. Howard was commanding the army that was trying to capture Chief Joseph and bring an end to the atrocities. Howard's location at the time was not known, but Will was sure that the general needed him as a scout. Nearly all the other men had families to care for and homes to defend, and were thus prevented from offering their services. Brother Van was also sure that he knew the country better than just about anyone else, and certainly far better than any of Howard's soldiers.

He had not yet had time to act on his resolve when word came to Bannack that the first major battle of the war had taken place on the Big Hole River. General Howard had been sent into Idaho to head off the uprising, if possible, and had met the Indians in several minor skirmishes, with no significant victories for either side. Chief Joseph, knowing that in open warfare he was no match for the U. S. Army, had conferred with his junior chiefs, Looking Glass and Blackbird, and had decided a running battle would work to their advantage. In this way, the 500 or so Nez Perce would be fighting Howard's horses more than his men, and Joseph knew the Indian ponies could outlast the cavalry horses. It was a brilliant strategic move, for part of

Howard's contingent were foot soldiers, and Joseph could, very literally, wear them out and run them ragged.

While the army had only its own forces, cannon, and supplies to move, Chief Joseph was moving his entire tribe— women, children, old people, the fighting men, and their tepees and meager supplies. This great running battle, beginning in Idaho, covered nearly a thousand miles before it ended in far northern Montana. The army would not have captured him then, except that Joseph mistakenly believed he had already reached the sanctuary of Canada, and was therefore legally out of reach of the United States' forces. That was why he had posted no guards to detect the approach of the U. S. Cavalry, which swooped to the attack on the peaceful Indian camp in the Bear's Paw Mountains, 50 miles south of the Canadian border.

Chief Joseph's generalship earned the praise of all who fought against him, and of those who heard of his exploits. General William Sherman of Civil War fame, who was the commander of all the forces in the West at that time, said Chief Joseph was the greatest general the world had ever known. By nature, he was not a fighting man. But when he was forced to fight, he proved himself to be anything but an "old woman."

Joseph had been correct in assuming that, even with women and children in tow, he could outrun Howard. But the wily chief had not counted on the telegraph as the most modern military weapon. By telegraph, the Indians' movements were relayed from fort to fort, and various contingents of troops were sent to intercept them. General Howard got word to Fort Missoula that the Nez Perce were leaving Idaho and were headed toward Montana's Bitterroot Valley, and would no doubt enter Montana by way of Lolo Pass. The commandant at Fort Missoula dispatched Captain Rawn and a small company of soldiers to intercept the

Nez Perce on the Montana side of the pass, and to engage them in battle until General Howard, returning from Idaho, could catch up and attack from the rear. It seemed like a good plan. But Chief Joseph outsmarted them.

We cannot imagine what type of persuasion he used, but the incredible fact is that when the army and the Indians met at the pass, the wily chief Looking Glass talked Captain Rawn into letting the tribe go though without a shot being fired! In the nearby town of Stevensville the Indians bought supplies, even including rifles and ammunition. This, too, quite defies explanation. It would appear the profit motive was alive and well in that day as in this. The merchant who provided the arms must have known they would be used against the white settlers, and that the profit he made from the sale would cost a goodly number of lives.

After obtaining their supplies in Stevensville, the Nez Perce band headed southward, toward the Big Hole River, at a leisurely pace, believing they had made good on their escape from General Howard. But once again they were betrayed by the telegraph. General Sherman ordered Colonel John Gibbon and a fighting force of 157 soldiers and 34 civilian volunteers to leave Fort Missoula at once, to move with all possible speed, and attack the Indians in the Big Hole basin. Colonel Gibbon's force sneaked into position under cover of darkness on the night of August 8, 1877, and just as the approach of dawn on August 9 made it possible to sight a rifle, he gave the order to open fire upon the slumbering, unsuspecting encampment.

Chief Joseph had not even bothered to post sentinels that night, knowing he had gotten well out of Howard's reach. Because there were no sentinels, Gibbon had been able to deploy his men in strategic positions on the surrounding hillsides, from whence their fire would converge on the Indians' camp from several directions. The first volleys of fire were disastrous to the Indians; in the dim light of early dawn, the soldiers shot at whatever they could see, and their bullets cut down women and children as readily as braves.

Quickly recovering from the surprise blow, The Indians took cover and sought more advantageous positions to defend. Although they outnumbered the bluecoats three to one, they were unable to launch a counterattack against the well-placed, dug-in troops. All of that day and throughout the night the battle continued. In order to obtain the element of surprise, Gibbon had left his artillery and his supply wagons three or four miles behind. On the morning of August 10, Gibbon found himself cut off from his supplies by a solid line of warriors. Sending out a party of soldiers to go to the rear and bring up a howitzer, Gibbon took a calculated risk—and lost. The Indians spied the group leaving the battle scene and laid down such a barrage of fire that they were forced to return to their line. The Indians then set fire to the grass and bushes in order to destroy the cover in which the soldiers were hiding, and perhaps to drive them out of their foxholes.

When a scout rode into Joseph's camp announcing that he had spotted General Howard not far away, the chief knew that the addition of Howard's men would turn the tide heavily in favor of the army. So, during the night of August 10, the Nez Perce withdrew, melting into the night, and pointed in the direction of Bannack.

Among the reserve forces coming in with General Howard was Major William A. Clark, later to become a U. S. Senator from Montana, and destined, too, to become one of the fabulous and notorious Montana copper kings. When Major Clark arrived, Colonel Gibbon said to him, "I tell you, major, we hadn't been in that battle but a short time when I thought it was going to turn into another Custer Massacre. There is only one reason, in my mind, why it was not. When we left Fort Missoula, the men were issued trowel bayonets.

These we used to dig holes into which we got for protection. If it hadn't been for that, none of us, in my opinion, would have lived to tell the tale."

Sixty of them did not live to tell the tale. Seven officers and 53 enlisted men were killed, and many others were wounded, including Colonel Gibbon, who took a bullet in the thigh. Indian casualties were not fully known, although 89 bodies were found in the area. Chief Joseph took all the wounded and very possibly some of the dead when he fled the scene of the battle.

When Brother Van got word of the battle up at the Big Hole, he knew that if ever General Howard needed him, it was now. Riding into Bannack Sunday morning to hold a church service, if possible, he found the town in an uproar. The Indians were headed toward Bannack, raiding as they came, and the people gathered in the town were, very appropriately, fearful and tense. Guards were posted on every hilltop around the town to give warning of anyone's approach from any direction. In the town, most of the people were gathered at the courthouse, which had been transformed into a kind of military headquarters. Around the building, barricades and other fortifications had been hastily constructed, behind which the citizens would do their best to repulse the expected attack.

It was getting toward evening before the situation had quieted enough for Brother Van to have a church service. That night, when the preacher said, "Let us pray," everybody really prayed. Brother Van implored God to spare them the waste and pain and death of battle. He spoke to them about life and death that night, and with the knowledge that some of them soon could fall before blazing Nez Perce rifles, his words about the Christian's victory in death took on a deeper meaning for the worshipers.

Sunday night in Bannack was sleepless, but it passed

without incident. And all was quiet until Monday noon, when a lone horseman was sighted by the scout on a hilltop just west of town. Several guns were trained on him, until he came near enough to be recognized as one of the settlers from Horse Prairie, a ranching region up against the foot of the mountains. The man was young, and as he rode up to the courthouse, they saw he was wounded. His right arm hung limp at his side, and his shirt sleeve was torn and matted with blood. Medical aid was immediately given; the wound was cleansed and dressed, and his arm was put into a sling. The bullet had torn muscle and flesh, but had not hit any bones, so the young fellow should mend well, it seemed. The freshness of the wound spoke more loudly than words could have as to the nearness of the Indians and their hostile disposition.

While that man's injury was being treated, another rider from Horse Prairie was admitted into town by the sentinels. The second rider turned out to be the man named Hamilton who operated the inn where Brother Van and Riggin had stayed on a few occasions. Hamilton told, breathlessly, how he had been racing ahead of a group of marauding Indians in his effort to reach the safety of the town, and how he had narrowly missed death at several points during his flight. Others, he reported, had not been so lucky. He told of a number of people out on Horse Prairie who had already been killed.

The Nez Perce were angered by the surprise attack of Gibbon in which many of their women and children had been killed and wounded, and were now, in retaliation, killing everything that moved as they pushed on to the southwest ahead of the pursuing U. S. cavalry and infantry.

The people gathered in Bannack knew Hamilton's story was true, because there were a number of the Horse Prairie folks not accounted for. They were not in the town, nor had they been seen recently by anyone. They were in mortal danger, if indeed it was not already too late to help them. In a hasty conference on the courthouse steps, it was decided that 15 men would be spared from the defense at Bannack, and that party would leave immediately on a dangerous mission to rescue anyone they could find alive on Horse Prairie. Brother Van was among the 15 who volunteered for the rescue party. He would not wear a gun, but in this case manpower was more important than firepower. Unarmed, he could still search for the missing and give aid to the wounded.

Saddling their horses and checking their weapons and ammunition supply, the group was ready to leave town when a pretty, dark-haired young woman approached Melvin Trask, the leader of the search party, and said to him, "Melvin, I'm going with you. My husband is out there on the ranch with our hired men. If he's in danger, I should be with him."

"I'm sorry, Mrs. Winter, but you can't go." Trask spoke in a tone of understanding and respect for the distraught young lady. "It's no place for a woman out there. We'll find your husband and bring him back to you. I promise."

Mrs. Winter protested bitterly, but Trask was intractable. Finally he spoke in desperation. "Mrs. Winter, the answer is still no, and I'm not going to let you hold us up any longer." He summoned one of the men standing guard nearby. "Frank, please take care of Mrs. Winter here. This is no trip for a woman, and that's that. Don't let her out of your sight until we get back from Horse Prairie."

Riding southwest from Bannack, the group of 15 had gotten about ten or twelve miles from town when they became aware of some rapidly-approaching hoofbeats. They dashed off the trail and hid in the brush to avoid detection, and were astonished, two minutes later, to see that the approaching rider was Mrs. Winter. Mounted on a beautiful strong horse, with her long black hair flying behind her, she made a spectacular appearance. Strapped about her dainty waist was a gun belt, and at her hip hung a large revolver which proclaimed that no power on earth was going to keep her way from her husband in his hour of peril. They asked her, of course, how she had gotten away from the guard, but she refused to tell them, not wishing to get the poor man into any trouble on her account.

Time was of the essence. They dared not delay the trip for hours in getting the woman back to town, so they had no choice but to let her proceed with them. Certainly they didn't dare to send her riding alone across the prairie back to town. Later, as the party rode up to the Winters' ranch house, Trask wished mightily he had made her go back, for it was not a pretty sight to behold. Even before they entered the yard, they could see the body of a man lying near the front door. Galloping ahead of the rest, Trask reached the gate. In a single motion he was off his horse and at the man's side. Bullet holes in his head were plain to see, and the man, of course, was dead. Mrs. Winter identified him as one of their hired men. Going inside the house, they found another body on the living room floor. It was Mr. Montague, who was in partnership with Winter on the ranch. Nothing more was in the house, and there were no signs or clues as to the whereabouts of Mr. Winter.

Next, the party did a thorough search of the farmyard and outbuildings. Beside the barn they came upon the lifeless form of another of the cowboys, and only a few feet away from him lay Farnsworth, the foreman of the Winter ranching operation. Farnsworth was still alive, but was so badly injured that he was unable to speak of what had taken place. Brother Van knelt in the dirt beside Farnsworth. Resting the victim's head in his lap, Brother Van offered a prayer for him. Before he had pronounced the "Amen," Farnsworth, too, was dead.

The Indians had been vicious and thorough. There were no survivors and no clues of the fate of Mr. Winter. Not knowing whether this ought to be considered good news or bad, Trask dispatched two of the search party to scour a couple of the surrounding hills and ravines to see if they could find anything. The two men were just out of sight when a group of Nez Perce braves appeared along the brush-lined creek just below the ranch house. From there, they began to shoot at the rescue party. While bullets whizzed around them, Brother Van and several other men loaded the four dead bodies onto horses, and the party made a hasty retreat out of the back yard, with Mrs. Winter showing them an alternate way out of their property. They left the two scouts they had sent out to fend for themselves. Those two men, of course, had heard the gunfire, and had gotten to a hilltop from which they could see what was happening. They took a circuitous route and soon rejoined the full party.

It seemed the part of wisdom to keep to low ground, since there were obviously hostile Indians very near. The last place they wanted to be was on a hilltop, in full view. They weren't far from the ranch when they rounded a bend in a ravine, and nearly ran over Mr. Winter, who was on foot, but alive and unharmed. After the ghastly scenes at the ranch, Mrs. Winter had been prepared for the worst, and had few hopes of seeing her husband alive. Her relief at finding him safe and sound was practically boundless.

The party made it back to Bannack without further incident, and the story of the killings at the Winter ranch and the rescue of Mr. Winter spread like wildfire through the town. Meanwhile, Brother Van was making arrangements for holding a quadruple funeral service. He was conducting the service for the four victims when a scout rode into the town, shouting, "The Indians are coming!" Brother Van hastily brought the service to a close, and everyone rushed to the spot he had been assigned to occupy in defense of the town.

People are fond of saying that it only happens in the movies that the cavalry rides to the rescue in the very nick of time to save the beleaguered settlers, but that is precisely what happened in the case of Bannack. Minutes after the first rider appeared, a second rider came into town, saying that General Howard had been spotted, just 12 miles behind the Indians. Fearing that Howard might be unaware of the plight of Bannack, it was agreed that if someone could get to him and advise him, he could come the rest of the way at a full gallop, and get to Bannack in time to meet the Indian attack head-on. Having Howard's soldiers added to the defending force at Bannack would change the complexion of the whole matter.

The difficulty with the matter was that in order to get to Howard, someone would have to ride right through the line of warring Indians. It was very risky, but someone would have to do it. Howard had to know what was going on in Bannack. At the call for a volunteer, John Poindexter stepped forward, and so did Brother Van. He told his friend, "If we both go, John, there's a pretty good chance of at least one of us getting through to Howard."

The two volunteers left town by way of the back door, so to speak. They made a large circle to the south, hoping to avoid an encounter with the band of Nez Perce, who were approaching from the west. When they thought they had circled far enough, they turned toward the north, knowing that up ahead they would either run into Howard's army or Chief Joseph's. They didn't much want it to be the latter. They had calculated correctly, for it was not long until they caught sight of Howard's limping infantry, and they quickly rode to the head of the line where the general was. Howard had not known the plight of Bannack and was quick to respond with help when John and Will told him what was needed. The army's principal duty on the frontier was to protect the settlers, so Howard instantly agreed to send a full company of cavalry into town with all possible speed. Brother Van and John explained to the captain who commanded the company exactly what route to take to get to the town without encountering the Indians, and the cavalry rode off to the rescue of Bannack.

It was apparent to Brother Van that Howard's army was in trouble. He still had some units that were fit and intact, such as the one he'd just now sent to Bannack, but Chief Joseph's brilliant and courageous maneuvers were taking their toll. His cavalry, men and horses alike, were worn out from the long and continued forced march in pursuit of the crafty Nez Perce. The infantrymen were in still worse condition. Some of the men were barefoot, their sturdy army boots having literally fallen of their feet from the constant abuse of climbing on rocks, fording icy streams and then baking in the hot August sun.

And Howard was in country he didn't know, cut off from his supply lines. With the Indians rampaging ahead of him, there was little left for his men to find in the way of food as the chase continued. This was the chance for which Will had been waiting, so he said, "General, it looks to me like you need a scout, and I'd like to volunteer. I don't think you'd find anyone who knows this particular country better than I do." John Poindexter said to Howard, "If you need two men, I'm also available." Finding two good scouts was like an answer to prayer for Howard, for a scout was one of the most essential men in a military operation. He gave the pair their first assignment at once.

The general urgently needed couriers to take important messages for the military headquarters in Washington, D. C., to the stage road which was not many miles east of Bannack. Once aboard the stage, the messages would be taken to the next point on the line where there was a telegraph, and from there they would be wired to Washington. Will and John agreed to take the hazardous ride. Leaving the army encampment at eleven o'clock that night, they hoped the remaining hours of darkness would cover their ride back to Bannack. From there it would be a simple matter to go east and meet the stage, for the Indians had not yet entered any territory east of Bannack.

Riding away from Howard's night camp, the scouts could hear the lonely hooting of an owl and the plaintive yelping of coyotes. In recording that experience, Brother Van wrote, "They are lonesome sounds at the dead of night under any circumstances, but when you know they are the signals of Indian scouts, they are simply hair-raising." Whenever they heard such a signal given, they tried to determine the direction from which it had come, and then they would ride for a time in the opposite direction. They figured they would encounter fewer Indians if they rode south for the first couple of hours and then headed east toward Bannack. Before making a move in any direction, they had to consider it well, because they knew that, in these circumstances, a mistake could be fatal.

By one in the morning they had been on the trail for two hours, but had gained very little distance due the constant changing of directions. Their hearts nearly stopped beating when they saw, in the pale starlight, the outlines of about 12 Nez Perce warriors not more than 50 or 60 yards ahead of them. Doing an immediate about-face as quietly as they could, Will and John scarcely dared to breathe while they rode away from the Indians. They were puzzled, and inexpressibly relieved, that the Indians did not pursue them nor shoot at them. Certainly the braves had seen them—they couldn't have been so unwary as to fail to observe two riders who were so near them. Probably the Indians were themselves a scouting party, and they didn't want to create a ruckus that would alert the army to their presence. They rode north for a little while and then turned back to the southeast until they recognized some landmarks that told them they were near Bannack. Then they headed due east, and before long they were at the stage road. Luckily, they only had a short wait until the very early morning stage came along. They flagged it to a stop, and gave the driver the military dispatch and the instructions to see that it got put on the telegraph at the first opportunity. The driver had been given such messages before, so he knew exactly how to handle this one. Their mission accomplished without mishap, General Howard's two scouts rode back to Bannack in time for breakfast. It had been a night to remember.

Things were now well under control in the little town. Howard's company of cavalry had arrived the night before and had manned the lookout posts, bringing enormous relief to the anxious and weary townspeople. Chief Joseph was too smart to take on a foe against whom he had no chance of victory. There was an army pressing him from behind, and a company of cavalry and several hundred local citizens with guns aimed at him in Bannack. Attacking a solitary and isolated ranch was one thing; taking on a whole city plus an army was quite another. Chief Joseph opted to bypass Bannack.

Will knew that Howard's forces would reach Bannack by the next day, and he would then be able to tell the general that he was resigning from his scouting duties. With the immediate threat of peril removed, Brother Van saw a unique opportunity that must not be allowed to pass by. The Indians were not attacking Bannack, but they were known to be still in the area, so it was not yet safe for the settlers to return to their ranches. There were several hundred people in town with nothing to do, but Brother Van had a cure for that in mind.

Before the Indian uprising, the people of the Bannack church, with Brother Van's leadership, had begun the construction of a church building. There was enough money in the building fund to buy the materials needed, so Brother Van circulated the word that there was going to be a great church-raising and anyone willing to work on it was welcome. The men in town, normally very active and hard-working, were going crazy from all the enforced inactivity of recent days, so they were delighted to have something to do. A large number responded to the call for workers.

Miners, cowboys, ranchers and soldiers all joined in the effort, and in record time the church building was completed enough to be used for a church service. That Sunday Brother Van preached the dedicatory sermon. Besides having the church dedication, there was also much to celebrate concerning the events of the past week. The dreaded Indian attack on Bannack had not taken place. While there had been, regrettably, a number of settlers killed in the outlying regions, the death toll was very small compared to what it might have been, and people felt both relief and gratitude.

Just the day before, word had reached Brother Van from the Methodist Mission Society in St. Louis that he was being assigned for temporary duty to do some work as a roving missionary for the Methodist denomination in the Bitterroot Valley of Montana. The Bannack dedication service thus became a farewell service as well. Saying goodbye to his many friends in Bannack, Brother Van left on Monday for the northwest, riding in daylight where, days before, he had feared to go even in the dark.

The route from Bannack to the Bitterroot led directly through the place where the Battle of the Big Hole had been so recently fought. Brother Van arrived there at the same time as a severe summer thunderstorm. There were great bolts of lightning and torrents of rain which forced him to set up camp for the night right there. He was able to hang a piece of canvas between some trees and huddled under it to keep the worst of the rain off him. He managed to start a fire, and occasionally ventured out of his shelter long enough to break some dead branches off the nearby trees for firewood. Anything lying on the ground was already well-soaked. It continued to rain, off and on, for two days, which gave him ample time to survey the battleground and try to reconstruct the scene in his mind. To his horror he found that the bodies of some of the Indians and soldiers who died there, having been hastily buried in very shallow graves, had been exhumed by wild animals. After he left the battle site, at his first opportunity he sent word of this to Fort Missoula, imploring the commandant there to send men down to properly bury the brave people, both Indian and white, who had lost their lives in the Battle of the Big Hole. The commandant took care of the matter at once, and said he appreciated Brother Van's reporting it to him.

At Skalkaho and Corvallis, two of the communities in Will's new parish, men were sent to the battlefield to bring home the bodies of local volunteers who had died fighting under Colonel Gibbon. When the men returned with the bodies, a great public funeral service was held, with Brother Van and other leading citizens taking part, to pay a fitting tribute to those who had died in defense of the homes of all the settlers. His first official duty at Sheridan had been to hold a funeral service; in the Bitterroot, history was being repeated. There was great sorrow in the community, for the dead at the Big Hole had included several of the finest young men in the valley. At this opportune time, when the promises of religion and the assurances of faith were much on peoples' minds, Brother Van began his Bitterroot ministry by holding a week-long revival, during which many souls were saved.

It is fitting, in recounting the life of this amazing and good man, to conclude a tale of horror, tragedy and bloodshed with the words "many souls were saved." To him, the only proper outcome for any venture, the only fitting climax to any story, and the only reason for undergoing any hardship was that souls might "come to Jesus," as he pled for them to do every time he preached.

Chapter Five

• • •

To the thousands who knew and
loved him all across the mountains, hills and prairies of
Montana, the pioneer parson was known affectionately as
"Brother Van." To the person who loved him most of all,
he was never Brother Van. "Will" was what Jennie always
called him.

When he was new as a minister in the Beaverhead Valley,
he had held a preaching service at the Poindexter school,
following which Mr. and Mrs. Richard Reynolds invited the
minister to be an overnight guest in their home. The three
children, who had remained at home, were all asleep by the
time the parents and their guest arrived home.

Brother Van, age 26 at the time, showed the usual
amount of interest he gave to children when Jennie, age 13,
came sleepily downstairs to breakfast the next morning. She
was a pretty, dainty, brown-eyed slip of a child, having the
face of a china doll, he thought. Her dark brown hair was
naturally curly but not luxuriously thick. It would have
hung down to her shoulder blades, but she kept it braided
and tied in a loose bun at the back of her neck.

Mrs. Reynolds felt it necessary to explain to Brother Van
how it happened that she was going by the name of
Reynolds, while her three children, Jennie, Georgia and

Philip, had the last name of Johnston. Something that cannot be explained is why Jennie always called herself Jennie Johnson, without a "t," when the fact is well-established that her name really was Jennie Johnston, with a "t." More likely than not, it was simply a matter of bowing to common usage. Since practically everyone naturally thought of it as Johnson, without a "t," she must have decided she would just go along with it instead of fighting it.

The lady who was now Mrs. Virginia Reynolds had been born a member of the Poindexter family. She married a physician, Dr. Oliver Johnston, who practiced family medicine in Danville, Missouri. To them were born a son and two daughters, Philip, Georgia and Jennie. Jennie, the youngest, was born on March 16, 1861, and she was very small when her father met an accidental death. Following the doctor's death, the widow brought her three children with her on a visit to the Beaverhead Valley of southwest Montana, where her brother, P. H. Poindexter, had come as one of the earliest settlers.

Mr. Poindexter, quite naturally, was eager to do all he could to help his sister in this very difficult time, so he urged her to bring the children and stay with his family as long as she wished. It proved to have been a good thing for her, since she soon met, fell in love with and married one of the stalwart young ranchers of the Beaverhead Valley, Richard Reynolds. Mr. Reynolds loved the three children and accepted them as his own, and they loved and respected him in return.

Jennie's mother and stepfather became very good friends with Brother Van, their minister, and always prevailed upon him to stay in their home when he was working in the Beaverhead. Theirs was one of those special homes that had a "Brother Van's Room." The preacher and Jennie, therefore, also had a very good relationship, but it was strictly on a platonic, brother-sister kind of basis—until 1879.

At the time of their first meeting, he was exactly twice her age, and at 13 she was merely a child. But that had been in 1874, and now it was 1879, and she was a young woman of 18. Brother Van, by that time, was 31, but the 13 years difference in age didn't seem to make such a great difference now. On the frontier, men were often quite a bit older than the women they married, so the age difference between Will and Jennie was nothing particularly extreme or unusual. Prior to 1879, it seems not to have occurred to either of them to think of the other as anything more than dear friends and fellow workers in the church.

But now the fact that Jennie was no longer a child, but had become a beautiful young woman came sharply to the preacher's attention. He was unaccustomed to having such powerful, distracting thoughts in his head, and they would not leave him alone, day or night. Was there any chance their long-time friendship could blossom into something more special? He simply had to know, before he lost his mind with wondering and hoping. Throwing his ministerial reserve to the wind, he wrote a 17-word message to her one morning from Sheridan, using the best grammar, spelling and punctuation he knew:

Sheriden March 17th, 1879

Miss Janie Johnson
My Sister in Christ.
    Can you think more of me than merely a Christian friend. Please answer in unhidden language immediately.

WW Van Orsdel

There! It was done, and within a week he should be advised what his chances were with Jennie. Meanwhile, he had his full round of ministerial activities to keep going. He addressed the envelope, sealed and stamped it, picked up his hat and strode purposefully out the door toward the post office. His message to her was certainly unmistakable; he hoped her reply would be affirmative and equally unmistakable.

Girls are most generally flattered to receive the attentions of males, particularly those of some prominence. Brother Van, of course, was widely recognized as the most eligible male in the entire Beaverhead, and most probably in a much larger area than that. He was loved and admired by people everywhere, who could not have helped but notice that he was unmarried, male, young, good-looking, interesting, kind and gentle—definitely husband material! Jennie was certainly not displeased to receive the terse, demanding note from Brother Van, but she had to be honest and admit that she had never permitted herself the luxury of indulging in any romantic daydreams that included him as the centerpiece. She replied to him:

> Beaver Head Co.
> Watson P. O.
> March 21st 79

Mr. W. W. Van Orsdel
Bro. in Christ:

Your very unexpected question is at hand and as you desire an answer immediately I take this my first opportunity to say that it would be impossible for me to give a direct answer, as I have never for a moment indulged any thoughts towards you other than as a dear Christian

Jennie Johnston. The only known photograph of the girl to whom Brother Van was engaged.

friend but I find in trying to examine my feelings I am prevented from saying, that I never can think any more of you.

I trust we may be guided in this matter, as well as everything else, by "His" divine counsel.

Jennie Johnson

Will guessed that this rambling, 94-word response to his simple 17-word question might be about as close as women come to speaking in unhidden language. While her letter left something to be desired, she had definitely left the door open, admitting that it might be possible for something to develop between them at some time in the future. Armed with this confidence, the young minister saw that the Beaverhead portion of his parish received much better than usual pastoral care in the next months.

When he was visiting at the Reynolds' home, the only place the couple could go to be alone was what they called "the white wickiup." A wickiup was a kind of Indian dwelling having a round or oval base, a framework of wood branches, and a covering of bark or grass. No descriptions exist of the wickiup on the Reynolds' ranch, but it was probably one erected some years before by a nomadic tribe of Indians. It was probably located near a creek bank, not far from the Reynolds' house. The time in the wickiup was very private and special, and nothing is revealed in any journals or letters of what went on between them on those occasions.

There is abundant evidence that as a result of their meetings and their private times in the white wickiup, their relationship grew into something far warmer than that between mere Christian friends. Less than three months after her first tentative, evasive reply, Jennie addressed a letter with the greeting "Dear Will," and said:

> I now find myself ready to say with more confidence that my feelings toward you are all that you desire and that I put the confidence in you that I have felt I never could in anyone else.

All that he desired! Will thought his heart would burst with joy when he read those welcome words. Again and again he read them, and it finally was accepted in his mind as reality. That was indeed unhidden language, for they had talked long enough and often enough that he was sure she knew that all that he desired was her lifelong, total love and commitment.

And Jennie had just told him that she was ready now to make such a pledge. For some time, Will had loved Jennie, and now Jennie also loved Will! Life was very good.

Fortunately, the letter had arrived at a time when he had no special or urgent commitments for a few days, so he saddled his horse and pointed it toward the Beaverhead. Will was not going to let this special moment pass. He always believed that the best time to do anything was right now. From the moment he started for the Beaverhead, the horse knew where they were going, and needed no guiding. This left the young parson's mind free during the many hours of riding, and in that time he prepared his next speech.

Brother Van spent his life giving speeches, but this would be the most important speech of his life, and he wanted to get it right. He was going to ask Jennie to marry him. As a poorly-paid clergyman who would always lead a somewhat nomadic existence, he didn't have a great deal to offer her except his love.

His promise of love was enough for Jenny. She accepted his proposal at once, but insisted that her parents must be consulted before any definite wedding plans were made. After dinner that evening, the parents and the young couple had a lengthy conference in the parlor.

Mr. and Mrs. Reynolds, of course, were very close friends with the minister in their own right. He was loved and accepted virtually as a member of the family already, and they knew their daughter could never marry a finer man than Brother Van, nor one who would love her more. But Jennie was already enrolled to attend Northwestern University at Evanston, Illinois, in September. Jennie's mother, in particular, felt that the girl should have an education, particularly if she was going to be the wife of a minister who would one day be a prominent public figure, as she believed Will was destined to be.

Jennie agreed with her mother's logic on that point. The conversation also brought to light the fact that Mrs. Reynolds had always regretted that she had married Dr. Johnston when she had been so immature herself. She was anxious to have Jennie mature a little more, so she could make the decision about marriage from a more adult viewpoint. She was, after all, a mere child of eighteen, who might be more infatuated than in love, and who might not be able to perceive the difficult role of a minister's wife in its true perspective.

Jennie was eighteen; Will was thirty-one. Jennie might have been a bit immature, perhaps, but he was ready for marriage *now*, and the thought of waiting for another year or two was decidedly unappealing. He favored learning, and he favored Jennie. Certainly he could not say, "I don't want Jennie to get an education," but he also could not say he would really be willing to wait another year or two to get married. But, when he saw that Mrs. Reynolds was not weakening in her resolve, and that Jennie also sincerely felt that a minister's wife should be a woman with an education, he relented.

He brought forth a counter-proposal. Whereas Mrs. Reynolds was pushing for two years of schooling and Will didn't really want her to go at all, if going meant the delay of their marriage, could they compromise and agree for Jennie to go to school for one year, after which the couple could get married? How about a wedding in the summer of 1880? While she didn't flatly reject the idea, Mrs. Reynolds would not openly accept it, either.

Brother Van was terribly upset, disappointed and dismayed at this turn of events. It is the only evidence on record of his having anything other than charitable feelings toward another person. Of course, there was not an open, red-hot, flaming battle over the matter, but in his letters to Jennie, Will obviously was burning with resentment toward Jennie's mother. They loved each other, had promised to marry each other, and wanted nothing more than to be together. Why should she keep them apart?

There is no doubt about it, if Jennie had been willing, Brother Van would have gone ahead and married her despite her mother's protest. Although she was only 18, Jennie was of legal age, and could have gotten married without her parents' consent. She was actually quite mature in her thinking for her age, Will thought. But she was unwilling to disobey her mother's wishes. Her loyalty to her mother and her love for Will presented some deeply confusing, conflicting emotions. She wrote to her betrothed at some length in this regard on August 14, 1879:

> It has been over a week since we parted—a week yesterday morning. I don't think I'll forget it soon—how hard it was to see you go without a chance to say anything but a formal 'Goodbye.' Ma has been gone to Argenta nearly ever since I got back. I felt like writing to you sometimes but then I wanted to have another talk with Ma first. So since she got back we have had a big 'Medicine Talk' which resulted quite satisfactorily I will give you a sort of outline—
>
> I explained as best I could how we both felt—that there should be nothing forced but that it should be perfectly satisfactory all around, in order to feel free and easy, as you had left it with me, and was as anxious as I was that she should be pleased. I wanted her to have her say how things should remain between us. at this she expressed her satisfaction at the way they were, provided we would wait some longer than the mentioned time. she talked more cheerful about it and more encouragingly than at any time before.
>
> I am sorry that she and you did not have more opportunity to talk together you would have understood each

other better. But now I want you to consider whether
or not I'll be worth waiting for?

I received a beautiful song book from (supposed to
be) unknown quarters. I prize it very much, it has a
double value, for you know if you'd written all day it
wouldn't have been half as expressive as those few little
words as they seemed to me when I read them over.

Yours as ever————
Jennie Johnson

Remember take care of yourself and watch out for Indians.

It is interesting to note that, despite the unquestionable fact
that Will and Jennie loved each other deeply and sincerely,
they were prevented by social custom and their own natural
reserve from making any overt display of it. Jennie infers
above that because her mother was present, she hadn't been
able to kiss Will goodbye, or at least hug him, when he left.
A voluminous file of letters Will and Jennie wrote to each
other fails to reveal even one time that either of them felt
free to say, in so many words, "I love you," nor did they
close their letters with love, or make use of any terms of
endearment, such as "sweetheart" or "darling."

Jennie's letters to Will typically begin with a greeting such
as "My dear Will," and are ended with "Your Jennie." His
letters to her follow an identical pattern. We know beyond
any doubt the two loved each other with all their hearts. It is
regrettable they could not put that affection into words. It is
to be hoped that in their private times together in "the white
wickiup" they may have been able to say words to each
other that they could not say under other circumstances.

Jennie and Brother Van's romance and betrothal was, of
course, the talk of the Beaverhead. Both of them were
beloved throughout the community, and everyone thought
they made a wonderful couple. Brother Van's virtues and

assets were well-known. And a lovely face was not Jennie's only virtue. All who knew her agreed she was a remarkable person of great spiritual depth and personal charm. She would make a very fine minister's wife.

The argument subsided, Round One having gone to Virginia Reynolds. Brother Van reconciled himself to having to wait for his beloved while she attended Northwestern for a year, or possibly longer. Despite having a spell of sickness in August, Jennie boarded the Beaverhead stage on September second, bound for Evanston.

She had written to Will just the day before, saying:

> I was up to Argenta the week before last—went on horseback and was sick for several days when I got back. It was pretty warm and I guess the ride was most too much for me. I feel first rate now though. . . .

She was accompanied on the trip east by her cousins, Minnie and Robert Reynolds, who were going to visit some relatives. The stage ride from Beaverhead to Corinne, Utah, wasn't as bad as it might have been; with eleven passengers, there was no room for them to be bounced around too much. At Corinne, they boarded the train, which was much more comfortable. Still, the trip was very taxing on Jennie. Minnie left the train at Ames, Iowa, to visit relatives, while Jennie and Robert went on to Kenosha, Wisconsin, arriving there exactly a week after leaving the Beaverhead. Kenosha, about 30 miles from Evanston, was the home of "Aunt Anne and Uncle Sam" Lane, relatives of Jennie's stepfather.

The Lanes were most friendly toward Jennie, demanding that she call them Aunt Anne and Uncle Sam, as the other young people all did. It distressed Jennie considerably, though, to learn that Uncle Sam had not the least interest in religion. He stayed at home, reading and dozing, while the rest of the family attended services.

After Aunt Anne had taken her on a whirlwind tour of Chicago, she and Jennie went to the campus of Northwestern. They arrived late on a Saturday evening, and Aunt Anne stayed the night with her. The little girl in Jennie was comforted not to have to face the new situation entirely alone. The next day being Sunday, they attended church together, and Aunt Anne helped her find her way around campus. By the time Aunt Anne had to leave, Jennie had already met a few of her new dormitory mates, and didn't feel so much alone.

The next couple of days were occupied in trying to get enrolled for classes. Problems in getting the classes one wants, it seems, are not a twentieth-century invention, as Jenny wrote to Will:

> the studies I was most anxious to take are not taught this term but there is plenty I'd ought to learn so it will be about the same. I dont care to take to much this term as I don't feel very strong. I have decided on two studies, with two hours of music practice a day and two lessons per wk. in a Normal class in which the method of teaching is explained. . . ."

Jennie found some of the 60 girls who lived in her dorm "pretty wild," but the girl who was her roommate was not one of those and became a very good friend.

Northwestern was, and is, a fully accredited university affiliated with the Methodist Church (now the United Methodist Church). Its mission was to provide the student with a first-rate education as well as to surround him or her with a wholesome Christian environment. Of that aspect, Jennie wrote to Will:

132

The teachers here at the school are all earnest Christians and try to use all the influence they can over the scholars in that direction. Our Dean Mrs. Bancroft who presides over the young ladies department is an excellent Christian lady who seems to take a special interest in each one of the girls. . . . We have a very interesting prayer meeting on Wed. Eve. in the building. I think it suits me as well as any place I could find so far from home. It is pretty expensive though it will hardly do for me to stay two years.

Such words gave Will new hope that perhaps the two-year sentence might be commuted to a lesser term. He certainly appreciated the value of an education, but he was human enough to put his heart before his head sometimes. He couldn't be blamed for thinking how wonderful it would be to have Jennie near him. He could imagine how grand it would be to come home from a hard trip and find her waiting in the parsonage.

At the risk of trying Jennie's patience to the breaking point, Will repeatedly asked in his letters how things stood relative to their plans for marriage. The reply was just as persistent: Mrs. Reynolds was still pushing for two years of schooling, and Jennie had not yet reached the point of being willing to go against her mother's wishes, despite occasional clues in her letters that her sentiments were swinging more in line with Will's.

Jennie knew, better than anyone else, that she was not in good health. As long as she was able, she continued in her classes at school, but her condition grew worse with each passing week. In early November, after about six weeks of classes, she finally had to drop out and consult a doctor. He advised her to take the medicine he prescribed, and to be careful not to overexert herself or get chilled. She checked

out of her dormitory and boarded a train for Kenosha, to
recuperate at the home of Aunt Anne and Uncle Sam.

It was only about an hour's ride to Kenosha, and when she
arrived there, Aunt Anne put her directly to bed. The next day
she was feeling a little better, and it was a warm day, so
cousin Charlie borrowed Uncle Sam's horse and buggy and
took her for a ride in the country.

Having to give up her studies was a terrible disappointment
to Jennie. Her marriage to Will had been postponed just so
she could go to school, and now she was neither married nor
going to school. But she wrote to Will in a philosophical vein:

> I feel there is one who knows the lessons I need better
> than I do, and I want to learn them in the right spirit.

It is a lesson she learned well, for throughout her long
ordeal of suffering, she remained serene and uncomplaining.

Nowhere is specific mention made of the exact nature of
Jennie's ailment. Most likely, she was a victim of tuberculosis.
In her letters there is some mention of coughing and in one
of his letters, Will asks if her lungs are still causing her pain.
If there were doctors anywhere who knew how to treat
tuberculosis effectively, she was never fortunate enough to
find one.

Jennie stayed at the Lanes and did her best to take care of
herself from mid-November until early February, venturing
out of doors only when the weather was very nice and there
was no danger of getting chilled. But despite taking all those
precautions and making sure to get a lot of rest, her condition did not improve. She had some good days, but there
was a gradual decline, she could tell, in her condition.

Christmas of 1879 was the bleakest one in Jennie's
memory. She was young, sick and away from home. The
Lanes were wonderful and kind to her, but they were not the

same as the home folks. Jennie got to go to a Christmas Eve party, and she was overlooked by Santa Claus. It was a trifle, to be sure, but to a lonely and frightened girl, it was calamitous. Such a thing could never have happened in the Beaverhead. Santa Claus always had something for everyone, and nobody was ever left out.

But harder things were still ahead. The Lanes could see she was not improving, and when she wanted to go to visit some Northwestern friends in Sturgis, Michigan, the Lanes allowed her to go, knowing the Battle Creek Clinic and Sanitarium was near there, and they believed that going there was her only hope. They made her promise that she would consult with the sanitarium, and check in there as a patient if it seemed to offer any hope of helping her. The Battle Creek Sanitarium had the reputation of having cured some seemingly hopeless cases. Their approach was unconventional, not relying on the use of medicines. Instead their treatments consisted of physical therapy, hydrotherapy, electric treatments and the like. Jennie had taken so much medicine in recent months that she feared developing a dependence on it. It didn't seem to be doing any particular good, anyway. She was concerned about her declining health and was ready to grasp at any new approach that seemed to hold promise.

So it was the first week in February 1880 that Jennie became a patient at the Battle Creek Sanitarium. Under their treatment, she felt that, at last, her health began to improve.

Brother Van, meanwhile, had been elected lay delegate from Montana (he still had not completed all the steps leading to full admission to the regular Methodist ministry) to the Methodist General Conference, the quadrennial business meeting of the national denomination. The conference would meet in Cincinnati, Ohio, for the whole month of May. He arranged his schedule so he could leave in plenty of time to do some visiting before the conference.

Tom Iliff, formerly of Montana, by now had been assigned to the Methodist work in Salt Lake City, so visiting with the Iliffs was Will's first order of business after he left Montana. Iliff insisted that Brother Van must stay the weekend, partly so the Montana pioneer could preach to Brother Iliff's Salt Lake flock, and partly so he could accompany Mrs. Iliff east on the train on Monday.

He would also be able, in this trip, to work in some all-too-brief visits with both of his brothers and one of his sisters. He stopped to see one brother for a few days in Estina, Nebraska, and while he was there, his other brother, who lived in Iowa, came over to join them, and the three Van Orsdel boys had a rollicking family reunion. Will and the Iowa brother went on to Iowa, staying a few days at that brother's home, and then Will went on to Tuscola, Illinois, to spend a week with one of his sisters. In Chicago, he had some official church business to take care of, and then he was ready to make his long-awaited visit to Jennie. Needless to say, neither one of them had been able to think of much else for quite some time before the visit.

The depth of love Brother Van felt for Jennie is perhaps best expressed in two statements he made in letters to her:

Next to Christian duty I have you on my mind more than anything else.

I am again writing to you on the sabbeth. As I have told you before I feel it is all right for me to write to you even if it is on the sabbeth. You are the only one I have wrote to on Sun. fore the last eight years.

Considering the source, this is a tribute of the highest order to Jennie. Christian duty was on his mind at all times, and the Sabbath was a sacred day, not to be profaned by any mundane activity.

It was three o'clock in the afternoon when the hack from the Battle Creek train station deposited Will at the front door of the sanitarium. Jennie had kept an anxious eye on the door ever since she awoke that morning. Despite her weakened condition, she managed to run to him, throw her arms around him, and the two held each other very close for a long time, as tears of joy streamed down both faces. They hadn't seen each other for more than seven months. Although they had corresponded frequently, there was still much catching up to do. By mail, you cannot hug and hold hands, and both of them were hungry for the other's touch.

Will was able to stay at the sanitarium as a guest through Sunday and Monday. Jennie, of course, continued to be subject to the rules for all patients. If the day was warm, she could go out for a buggy ride for an hour or two in the afternoon. She had to be in bed by eight o'clock at night, and couldn't do much else but stay in bed and rest. Most of the hours they had together were spent in her room, holding hands, talking of their future together. Will, of course, caught her up on all the happenings in Montana that were of interest to her.

They had something important and new to put on their agenda for conversations, because Brother Van had stopped to have a visit with Jennie's mother and stepfather not too long before his trip to see Jennie, and Mrs. Reynolds had written to her daughter stating that all restrictions on her marriage to Brother Van were lifted, and the two were to be allowed to work it all out in their own good judgment. The couple talked extensively about the freedom they now had to get married, and they spent many happy hours dreaming dreams and making plans for the future that would be theirs. When the time came for Will to leave, both of them were more confirmed than ever in their love.

However optimistically she wrote and talked, Jennie was

not getting better. She didn't complain, but the gravity of her condition is revealed in such statements as the following:

> I intended to write to you sooner, but there was an
> urgent letter I had to write to Ma, and I didn't feel able
> to write another letter on the same day.

Another time she explained that she was "Not so well and writing was to much for me."

Her discouragement grew, and she said, "I don't pretend to say how I am by how I feel." One day she would feel reasonably well, and the next day she would be laid low again. She began less often to speak of returning to health.

It didn't help Jennie's state of mind to be the principal witness to a suicide attempt one morning as a fellow patient leaped over the fourth floor balcony, falling to the first floor. The poor woman wasn't killed in the fall, but she died several days later.

Virginia Reynolds was becoming alarmed about Jennie's condition, and she talked of coming out to Battle Creek to see Jennie and, if possible, to take her home. Jennie sensibly felt it was best for her to remain at the sanitarium a while longer to see if their treatments helped, and that a trip by her mother would be expensive and couldn't actually accomplish anything. She dissuaded her mother by saying that in a couple of months she would leave the sanitarium and come home.

A certain Doctor Kellogg, who may or may not have been affiliated with the Kellogg Sanitarium, but probably was, gave a series of lectures for the patients on the topic of "How to Get Well." He made the extravagant and ridiculous claim that anyone who desired good health could have it. Jennie and other patients came to his talks with great hopes, but were disappointed. Nobody desired good health more earnestly than she, nor had better reasons for wanting and needing it. She followed to the letter all the professional advice she was given, but nothing helped her to get better.

In July, Jennie decided to leave the sanitarium. For nearly three weeks she stayed with her friends at Sturgis, the adjacent town, and on the first of August she returned to Kenosha to the home of Aunt Anne and Uncle Sam Lane. After lengthy discussion and debate, it was agreed that Aunt Anne would go to Montana with Jennie. Jennie protested that she would be able to make the trip just fine unaccompanied, but the Lanes wouldn't hear of it. Jennie was more seriously ill than she was able to tell, or more than she was able to admit to herself, but others could see how she was declining. That Mrs. Lane was making a trip to the wild and far-off country of Montana made a great impression on all the local friends and relatives, and during the last couple of days before the trip, everyone came by to wish the travelers well.

The trip home proved to be pleasantly uneventful, and they reached the Beaverhead almost exactly a year to the day from the time Jennie had left. Of that year, only about 6 weeks had been spent in school; the other 46 weeks had been devoted to her unsuccessful attempts at convalescence. She couldn't regret the time too much, though, for she had learned a few things in her very brief educational venture. She had made new friends, become acquainted with loving new relatives, and had seen a lot of interesting new places. Growing up in the Beaverhead, she had heard of the world that lay beyond, and now she had seen a small part of it.

A week of continuous travel is difficult even for a person in good health, so it is not surprising that Jennie arrived home somewhat the worse for wear. After a few days of complete rest, she felt better. It was so good to be home! She could relax and rest, and sleep, as she had not been able to do for a year. Here, in these familiar surroundings, she felt totally safe and secure. She regretted she had not made the decision to leave the sanitarium much earlier.

Brother Van had a large parish and a busy schedule, so Jennie knew she could not expect to see him too frequently. Still, it was a great comfort to know he was not many miles away. He kept her informed of his schedule of appointments as best he could, and he came to see her whenever it was possible to make even a momentary stop in the Beaverhead. Upon a couple of occasions, when he was at some point not far away and the day was warm enough to permit an outing, Jennie went to see him.

For several months after her return home, Jennie's health appeared to improve considerably, at which Brother Van and her family felt greatly encouraged. In February of 1881 she caught the measles and apparently didn't have much trouble with them, which testifies to her increased strength at that time. In the weeks that followed, several other family members had the measles, and Jennie helped to take care of them.

Nobody had ever said what was actually ailing Jennie, and at that stage in our country's medical development, there were few medications available that actually had any curative powers, if her illness had been precisely known. The only thing Jennie knew to do for herself was to get lots of rest, stay warm, and take her cod liver oil.

In the late spring of 1881, Jennie's condition began to deteriorate more seriously. A letter she began writing to Will on Monday was not finished until Wednesday; she was so weak she could only write a few lines at time. On Monday, June 27, Jennie's mother wrote a letter to Will in which she expressed her great concern over her daughter's condition:

June 29th, 2 o'clock (1881)

Dear Brother Van Orsdel,

Jennie wrote a few lines, so I will add a few more. I think she is improving slowly. She still continues to eat quite hearty, has not much pain in lungs—a good deal of other pain, but I think her spells are not so often. Slept well last night—her cough is very loose today and it does not exhaust her so much to cough as it did. It does seem now as if she would certainly recover. I wrote to Leavitt again today in regard to the pain, hope he can help her more than he has done. I did not let her see the enclosed letter from him. I do not know if he fully understands the case, but I am sure she seems better, and I do not at present think the case hopeless. God grant it. I thought I would write to Mrs. Lane all about the case, and send the letter of Leavitt's and get her to consult the physician that attended Jennie there, and if he could advise me by letter, it might be some benefit, *What do you think.* Please send the letter to me in Mrs. Jane Selway's name. I can get it from there, as I do not wish to risk it getting to Jennie, for she always watches so closely for the mail. Hoping that you will have as good a time as you can under the circumstances, I remain your Sister in Christ———

V. E. Reynolds

The identity of Leavitt is unknown. Apparently he was a physician, not from the Beaverhead, who had done some consultation on the case, and had written a letter to Mrs. Reynolds expressing his belief that Jennie's case was hopeless. Naturally, they would not want Jennie to read her own death sentence, nor did they want to accept it as the final verdict themselves.

141

Later the same day Jennie wrote to Will:

I was going to write a few words this morn in Ma's
letter but sleep overtook me before the materials were
brought but I start in now to have this ready for next
time. Trying to be a good girl since you left keep my
weak side covered pretty well and take my cod liver oil.

There she stopped and on Tuesday she resumed, referring
to the letter her mother had written to Will:

I guess you have been well informed how I have been
getting on up to yesterday. I did pretty well yesterday
on the whole but had several *spells* some with my lungs
which I think some better today. very sore though.
   Did not have a very good night last night so am more
tired and weaker on account.
   I was happy on receiving your letter today. O Will I
do miss having you here ever so much.
                                          Your Jennie

Wednesday morn: feel better than usual this morning
and happy.

Reading between the lines, Will understood that by now
Jennie was completely bedfast, even having to have writing
materials brought to her. When he went to see her in July, he
was shocked to see how much weaker she had grown since
he had last seen her. He was in great despair to see his
beloved Jennie slowly but surely losing her life in this grim
struggle, nullifying all their plans and dashing all their hopes.
It was almost more than he could bear. He loved her so
intensely, and there was nothing he could do to share her
pain or ease it. He longed to be with her, but when he was

at her side, he was scarcely able to control his grief. These
days would remain with him always as his personal
Gethsemane—his darkest hour of trial.

Everyone in the valley knew about Jennie's perilous condition, and it was of real personal concern to them, too. Early
on the morning of July 16, the Reynolds were awakened by
their neighbor, Mr. Axe, who had found a doctor traveling on
the stage toward Helena and had persuaded him to lay over
until the next stage so he could come and examine Jennie
and see if he could possibly help her.

Following a lengthy and seemingly competent examination,
Doctor Parcher said he considered her main problem to be a
malfunctioning liver. He advised her not to drink beer (as if
she ever had!). He also said she had taken a lot of medicines
she'd have been better off without. He couldn't offer any
help, though. The best advice he could give was for her to
get complete bed rest.

After July there are no more letters at all, testifying that she
was too ill and weak to write, and Mrs. Reynolds was too
busy caring for Jennie to have time to write. It is possible,
but seems unlikely, that Will may have gotten letters right up
to the last which were so full of pain for him that he
couldn't bear to keep them. He did re-arrange his schedule
during her last weeks, so that he could get to the Beaverhead
more often to pay her a short and painful visit.

Calling on the sick is part of the minister's daily routine,
but visiting Jennie was the hardest thing Will had ever done.
He loved her very much, and he could hardly bear to see the
suffering she was experiencing. The pain was multiplied by
the fact that, as he saw her in the process of dying, he knew
that all his fondest dreams were also dying. The wonderful
life together which they had planned would never become a
reality. Many times he wished that they had refused to abide
by her mother's demand that they postpone marriage while

Jennie went to college. At least, in that way, they would have had a few months of married happiness before Jennie became too ill. He never revealed to Jennie that he had entertained such a thought; it would have been a cruel hurt to her to make her deal with such an idea. He wondered if she had ever had the same thought, but knew it wasn't worth bringing up. What's past is past and cannot be undone.

Mrs. Reynolds sent a message on the Beaverhead stage to Brother Van in Sheridan about the fifteenth of October, telling him that they didn't believe Jennie could live many more days. Will hastily rearranged his schedule to permit him to go to the Beaverhead, hoping he would arrive while Jennie still lived.

He got there in time, but Jennie was sleeping or unconscious most of the time, and too badly wasted away to be able to communicate. She had always been a rather diminutive person, and the months of illness had taken a dreadful toll. It was hard to believe it was really Jennie lying there. She did seem to waken, briefly, and Will felt her grip his hand more firmly as he stood helplessly at her bedside, weeping. He was convinced she knew it was her beloved who was holding her hand as she drew her final, troubled breath and died.

Time stood still for Will on October 20, 1881, when Jennie was taken into that brighter world in which she so strongly believed. He could not wish her back, to resume her pain and suffering, but he didn't know how he could go on living without her. He had loved her so very much, and the two of them had such great plans, but, as he so often said, "Man proposes, and God disposes." Perhaps in some way Jennie's death made sense to God; it didn't make sense to him.

On the day of Jennie's funeral, Will went into the parlor to be alone with Jennie one last time before she was laid to rest.

He sobbed uncontrollably for awhile, and then he caressed her cold cheek with his fingers and prayed, thanking God for the love and joy Jennie had brought into his life. He took from his coat pocket the ring he had bought months before, to give to her in their marriage ceremony, lifted her unresponsive hand, and slipped the ring on her finger. She would, after all, wear his ring for eternity. And perhaps, in the sight of God, they were man and wife.

Life goes on, of course, and Brother Van's life was to last many more years. He would do important and interesting things in years to come, and he would once again laugh and sing. Still, there can be no doubt that a part of him died with Jennie. He never forgot her, and she always remained his one and only love. While she lived, he had frequently plucked wild roses as he rode along the trail and pressed them into his letters to her. Now, whenever he was in the Beaverhead, he went to her grave, knelt in prayer, wept a while, and left an offering of flowers. He paid homage to Jennie as long as he lived.

If there was a purpose to Jennie's death, perhaps it was that she had to die in order for Will to become the Brother Van who made such a lasting impression on Montana. He remained unmarried all his life, and thus was always free to travel to every section of the state, going from place to place to place, and rarely going home in between. Testifying to his relentless pursuit of duty is an article that appeared in a Fort Benton newspaper: "Brother Van is supposed to have a room in Great Falls and a place whereon to lay his head, but he tells us that in the last month he has slept in 29 different beds, while his own has been unruffled." This was not an unusual month, but was in fact quite typical of the schedule he maintained throughout the 29 years he served as presiding elder and district superintendent.

It would have been a lonely life for a woman, being the

wife of such a man. Or, in order to establish a reasonable kind of home and family life, he would have had to literally "change his spots," and could not have become the Brother Van of history. He wrote in his journal on New Year's Day, 1894, "I consecrate my all to thee O Christ at the dawn of the new year." It was a yearly pledge he never failed to keep. Except for his singing ability, Brother Van was quite an ordinary man, but he had such extraordinary faith, zeal and commitment that he seemed to be a superman. The Lord and the church had all there was of Will Van Orsdel in every respect. There wouldn't have been much left to give a wife.

However much the church and state may have gained by Brother Van's long life of bachelorhood, we cannot refrain from mourning with him the death of Jennie Johnston. With the abiding love they had for each other, it is a pity they were not permitted to have a life together, build a home and raise a family.

He wrote in his 1881 journal: "Jennie Johnson went to her long home safe in the arms of Jesus, Oct, 20, 1881. Dear girl, you are not forgotten." His 1893 journal entry for October 20 says, "12th anniversary of Dear Jennie's death. O what changes these years have brought."

Brother Van lacked no confidence in the Christian doctrine of immortality, but he had a very understandable human desire for love and companionship; a need which, in his mind, only Jennie could ever have filled.

Chapter Six

• • •

*B*rother Van's activities had been arduous while Jennie was alive; inspired by romance, he made sure he spared no effort in doing such a good job that she would be proud of him. After her death he dug in with renewed fervor, perhaps in the hope that by losing himself in his work he would have less time to be conscious of the great ache in his heart and the yawning void at the center of his life.

For part of the year prior to Jennie's death, he had been doing missionary work, and had established several new churches in the Sun River area where he had been so warmly welcomed by the Bulls about nine years before. Some of the communities (which he referred to as "preaching points") had been visited by traveling preachers before, but none had ever come with the intent of establishing a church. For the church to exist, there must be more than a periodic preaching service; there must also be a Sunday school and the historic rites and sacraments, and these must be available on a continuing basis to serve the peoples' needs.

There was no shortage of work to be done, for in all of Montana there were dozens upon dozens of similar communities or regions, all having the same need for the presence of an established church. The Methodist bishop, I. W. Joyce, said of Montana at about this period, "I have been all over the world, and I find in Montana a larger percentage of college-bred men and women than anywhere else on the frontier. I also find a larger percentage of backslidden Congregationalists, Baptists, Presbyterians and Methodists than elsewhere."

Circuit riding was Brother Van's particular forte; he was never fond of the notion of settling down in just one place as a pastor, and preaching to the same people several times a week. He was very good at doing shorter stints, such as a week or two of revival services, and holding enough services and business meetings to get a church established, but then he wanted to be pushing on to other places. While he was organizing a church, he kept closely in touch with his presiding elder and bishop, and as soon as they could find a preacher to send to the charge, Brother Van would be off to the next place where he intended to organize a congregation and establish a church.

This is not to infer that he lacked concern for and interest in these new congregations. Seldom has there been a minister more sincere in his purpose. His journal entry for November 23, 1879, tells of the founding of the new church at Chestnut in these words:

> The grate head of the church was present and we had a good time. I pray that these churches may be as trees planted by the riverside.

As popular and beloved as he was, he was presented with a good many opportunities to settle down as a local pastor. When the people at Helena invited him to become their pastor, he declined, with thanks, and wrote in his journal:

. . . they have asked that I be sent here as pastor. I am shure they don't know me or they would not ask fore that. I am to ignorant and weak for such a position.

He was always, at heart, a missionary at large. He was the right man in the right place at the right time for the work that needed to be done in Montana. Whenever he found a group of people interested in having a church in their community, he went to work and got it done, even if it wasn't strictly within his assigned area. Throughout his life he lived by the philosophy, "a church in every community, and a yearly revival in every church."

A kind of "second phase" of the settlement of Montana was taking place. The days of the early pioneers were history. The gold rush was over, Jennie was a painful memory, the settlers and Indians were living together quite peaceably, and the territorial capital had been moved from Virginia City to Helena in 1875. Now the agricultural and industrial settlement of Montana was beginning, and Brother Van was bringing the church to isolated ranching and mining regions. He was there ahead of any other church, and even ahead of most of the people.

In the geographic heart of Montana is a region known as the Judith Basin, which extends, roughly, from the present towns of Lewistown on the east to Belt on the west, a distance of nearly 100 miles. In those early days, the area was important both for ranching and mining, as it continues to be today. It was one of those places at which Brother Van arrived ahead of the rush of settlers; his ministry and the churches he founded grew with the country. In his own handwriting we have the account of his first visit:

I made my first trip into the Judith Basin on horseback, August, 1882. Stayed all night at the Severance ranch, about six miles south of Judith Gap, where the Barrows road house was then. Great excitement prevailed because the Indians had run off some horses the night before. At this time I met Mr. Morrison, proprietor of the new town of Philbrook, about 30 miles north. He gave the new hotel building, which was almost completed, for us to hold services in the following sabbath. There was a large turnout, the settlers coming from many miles in several directions to attend the first preaching service ever held in Fergus County. The small daughter of Clarence Barnes was baptized, and this was the first baptism ever performed in that area.

From there I went to Pig Eye Basin, where I met C. C. David and family, about 18 miles from Philbrook. I met Sister David some distance from the house. She was afoot, looking for the horses, which it was soon learned the Indians had stolen. From there I crossed the Belt Mountains and spent the next sabbath at Barker, where I held services that morning and evening. From there the next day I went to Neihart where I held a service that evening. At that time, no ladies had ever been in that town. There were about 20 men in the mining camp, all of whom were at the service.

The important difference between Brother Van and other traveling evangelists was that after he preached and issued a plea for sinners to repent, he also issued a plea for funds with which to build a church and parsonage. Donations were garnered in a miraculous way, when one considers that most people in those times were hard-pressed for cash. The first, and very often the largest, donation to each building crusade was Brother Van's own. No one knows how many thousands of dollars, over the years, he invested in the churches and the Methodist institutions that he brought into existence, but it would be quite a staggering sum.

Brother Van was not a tither—one who gives a tenth to the church. He was probably a "reverse tither," using for himself about a tenth of his income. His way of thinking was not "How much of my money shall I give to the Lord?" It was "How much of the Lord's money shall I use for myself?" It was said that Brother Van's pockets leaked. If he had a little money, it didn't take long to find someone who needed it more than he did. A friend in Fort Benton gave him a nice pair of mittens one winter, and Brother Van was very pleased to get them. But the first time he wore them, he saw a man who was down on his luck who didn't have any mittens. The mittens then became a gift for the second time in their very short life.

Having no wife or children to support, no home or auto to maintain, a free pass to ride the trains, and free room and board everywhere he went, he could live on surprisingly little cash, and he did. Most of what he received as income was available for charitable work, and he found great satisfaction in being able to make significant contributions to help start churches, build parsonages and establish important institutions.

At most of the places where he preached, he either found or created through conversions in his preaching services a handful of devoted Christian people who could be relied upon to keep a Sunday school going in his absence. It was always a big day for that community when Brother Van returned to sing and preach and help with the Sunday school. It was just as big a day for Brother Van, who thrived on such occasions.

Each of "his" churches seemed like his own offspring, and his pride in them was boundless. It was one of the joys of his life to go from town to town, revisiting churches he had established. Seeing a small, plain, one-room wood frame building with its spire holding a cross above the plains, he would say to whoever may have been with him, "There's the church. Isn't it beautiful?" To him, they were truly beautiful. To the casual observer it may have seemed to be the plainest box-like structure; to him it was magnificent. He was never much impressed with stained glass, gothic spires and pipe organs. The world's great cathedrals, to him, were the tiny churches of log or wood frame construction which dotted the plains, mountains and valleys of Montana in the wake of his visitations and ministry.

It grated on Brother Van's nerves to hear ministers speak of their church as a "plant." To him, it sounded irreverent, worldly and crude, as though the church were a factory which produced Christians on an assembly line. The church was the house of God, whether it held 20 or 2000 persons, and its facilities were designed as a meeting place between man and God.

Jennie was the only woman in Brother Van's life, but there were two men, in particular, with whom he shared his life in a deeply significant way: Dr. Thomas C. Iliff and the Reverend Francis Asbury Riggin. He loved and was loved by innumerable other men and women, but none were as intimately acquainted with him or related as closely with him as Jennie, Tom and Francis.

One of the happiest associations of Will's life was developed in the earliest trail-riding days with Thomas C. Iliff. The two were alike in many respects, and yet different in enough ways that they very nicely complemented each other. Together, they made a powerful team that came to be known nationally as well as in Montana as "the heavenly twins." Iliff had come to Montana more than a year in advance of Brother Van, and his first work was that of establishing a Methodist church in Missoula, the major city of western Montana. In 1871 there was little at Missoula other than the military garrison of Fort Missoula, about 4 miles from the townsite. Dr. Iliff and his wife were excellent workers who quickly won the hearts of the people, and the local populace responded by generously supporting the effort to build a new church.

Will first met Iliff at Sheridan in 1873, on the same day he met Francis Riggin. Iliff was one of the ministers returning from the Annual Conference in Salt Lake City, all of whom had stopped over at Sheridan to see Brother Van and Riggin installed in their new joint ministry. Tom Iliff had just been assigned to the Bozeman circuit, making him their nearest neighboring pastor. Will and Iliff developed a warm friend-ship and worked cooperatively on revivals as often as possible.

Tom Iliff was a colorful character who grew to national prominence in the Methodist Church. And Mary Iliff was a wonderful woman, equal to the hardships that were the usual lot of a frontier pastor's wife. It is entirely possible that one of the reasons Will was so eager to be married to Jennie was the love and warmth he observed in the Iliff home. He wanted to have a home like that, too.

One day in 1873 a band of Nez Perce Indians came through Bozeman on a hunting expedition, far afield from their Wallowa Valley home in Idaho. They were not on the warpath against whites at that time, but Mary Iliff was nonetheless terribly frightened one day when she was home alone, and Amos, the chief medicine man of the Nez Perce, entered her home without knocking (Indians never knocked). She had read tales of the savagery of Indians, and had heard many first-hand accounts of people being attacked, kidnapped or killed by them. Naturally, she was terrified to see the man in her house, and wondered what fate was to be hers. After much grunting and gesturing by Amos, she came to understand that he simply wanted her to boil the 4 or 5 dozen eggs that he had in a dirty burlap bag. Mary was quick to comply with this simple request, and didn't bother to ask how he had obtained them. She and Amos stood wordlessly by the stove while the eggs cooked. When they were done, she drained off the boiling water, poured some cold water over them to cool them, and gave them to Amos. He put them back in the bag and left as quietly as he had come.

Mary had just about forgotten that unusual experience by the time Amos returned, again entering the house without knocking, some days later. She recognized him, of course, and had heard that the Indians had gone toward Yellowstone Park to do their hunting. As before, he carried the same dirty burlap bag, and Mary assumed he had some more eggs to be boiled. Instead, with a great flourish, and using all the English he knew, Amos reached into the bag and said. "Present! Kill Sioux, take scalp. Present!"

She feared she would faint from the wave of nausea that came upon her as Amos' hand came out of the bag, clutching six gory, matted Indian scalps. Instead, Mary bravely affected an air of great delight and took the scalps the Indian shoved into her trembling hand. Despite her shocked state, she managed to mutter some words of thanks, which Amos, of course, could not understand. The fact that she held them indicated she had accepted the gift. Mary knew enough about Indian ways to understand that a man's rank in the tribe depended upon the number of enemy scalps he had. They were considered of greater value than buffalo robes, horses or jewelry. Amos was repaying her in an extremely generous and absolutely unique way for her small kindness in boiling the eggs for him. In more ways than one, it was a truly staggering gift.

What does one do with a gift of six Sioux scalps? Repulsive as they were, she also understood how extraordinary they were. Later, the scalps were used in a remarkable way. The famed Chaplain McCabe, whose lecture on Libby Prison Will had gone to hear in Chicago, was Mrs. Iliff's cousin, and he was still on the lecture circuit. When he heard from cousin Mary about the Indian scalps, he asked if he could borrow them for a few months. Mary was glad to have them off her hands, and sent them to him. He put the six scalps on a stringer and waved them before audiences all across America as the chief stage prop in his dramatic presentation of the need to build the church out West and bring an end to savagery. The scalps later played another important role when Dr. Iliff was transferred to Salt Lake City in order to build a church there. The six Sioux scalps, sold at auction, brought in the $25,000 that was needed to complete the building of the first Methodist Church in Mormon country.

When he had first come out West, Iliff had been assigned to a rather large parish. Specifically, his orders instructed him to go to the Rocky Mountain country, and to view Canada, Mexico, the Missouri River, and the Pacific Ocean as the boundaries of his parish. John Wesley, the founder of Methodism, was supposed to have said, "The world is my parish." Tom Iliff could almost have said that half the continent was his parish. Deciding for a time to settle at Missoula, Iliff was distressed to learn there was quite a large number of hostile Indians in the area. At his suggestion, a company of local volunteers was organized to supplement the soldiers at Fort Missoula in the protection of the populace.

Nearly every evening that he didn't have church duties, Tom Iliff could be found in the village square, drilling the recruits. When General James Garfield (later President) came to inspect the fort, he heard about Iliff's activities and went to see the minister. Garfield said, in a caustic manner, "I

thought you were sent out here to save souls, not to shoot
Indians! I mean to talk to your bishop about this when I get
back to Washington, young man!"

"I dislike to remind you, general," Iliff retorted hotly, "that
we have to save their bodies before we can save their souls."

Iliff was a fiery and turbulent man, immensely persuasive. It
was said of him that "as he spoke, from the hot cauldron of
his being, body, mind and soul, his eloquence bubbled,
effervesced, and finally overflowed his hearers until they were
completely in rapport with him and whatever cause he
represented." At the Methodist General Conference in
Saratoga Springs, New York, the Heavenly Twins were in
great demand for services of sermon and song. One book
says of them, "Brother Van could stir that great aggregation
of cosmopolitans at any hour or in any turbulent juncture
with Dr. Spencer's hymn, 'Harvest Time,' while Dr. Iliff's
stentorian shout and perennial blaze of spiritual energy would
have the perturbed host joining with him in fervent tears and
hallelujahs."

Brother Van and Tom Iliff faced, alone and together, some
very tough congregations. When Iliff founded the Methodist
church in Missoula, it was the only one between Helena and
Walla Walla, Washington. In Missoula, he soon learned the
meaning of the term, "the wild and woolly west."

He started the church-establishing effort in Missoula by
holding a revival, and on the opening night things went
smoothly enough. On the second night, ten men wearing
revolvers entered the room where the services were being
held and indicated by their actions they were taking charge,
and they hadn't come tonight to worship. While Iliff
attempted to open the service with a prayer, they drowned
the sound of his voice by hooting, jeering and swearing.
Knowing he could not compete with the ruffians, Iliff
adjourned the meeting, telling everyone to return the next

evening. Nothing could have served better to stimulate attendance for the next night, as the whole town was engaged in speculating all that evening and the next day what the rowdies would do and what the preacher would do.

That night, when he adjourned the meeting, Tom Iliff didn't know what he would do. He thought and prayed about it that night, and by morning he had a plan. He didn't have to go far around town until he found the man he was looking for. Bill Burmeister was a renowned gunfighter and was noted for many things, of which religious fervor was not one. But he did have a sympathetic ear for the pastor's story. Burmeister knew that group of trouble-makers, and thoroughly disliked each one of them. He was openly pleased to have an opportunity to stand up to them and display his authority as a gunman.

Bill said, "Reverend, I haven't been to church once in 27 years, but I'll do this chore for you on one condition—that you leave it all to me and let me handle it my way. Agreed?"

"Agreed!" Iliff was immensely relieved to have the problem off his hands. He didn't much care how Burmeister handled it, just so he did handle it.

Burmeister quietly rounded up a dozen of his gun-toting friends and told them they were all going to church that night, and they should wear their guns. They came early and took up positions all around the room. Each man had a gun; several had revolvers hanging at both hips. That night, when the ten ruffians entered the room where the church service was to be, they saw Burmeister and his men, and immediately decided they would worship elsewhere that night. "I guess the trouble's over, Bill," the preacher said. "You and your men don't need to stay, unless you want to." Most of the men left, but Bill stayed, and before the series of meetings ended, he was converted. The rowdies never bothered Iliff's services again, apparently convinced that a preacher who had command of a bunch of gunslingers was not an appropriate target for their harassment.

Mention was made in an earlier chapter of the time when Brother Van and Riggin invited Iliff to be the guest preacher at a series of revival meetings in Virginia City. That revival was a great success, and Billy Blay was the main reason.

Billy Blay was the worst sot in a town that was known for them. Deciding the evangelistic mission needed to direct its efforts at the town's toughest cases, Will and Tom went to the filthy hut where the drunkard lived for that little part of the time he was not in a saloon, and spoke to him about the merits of the Christian life. They talked a bit, and prayed aloud for Billy, but there was no indication of response from him. The two young preachers understood now what the people meant who had told them that Billy Blay was the toughest case in Virginia City for them to tackle. For several days in a row they came to Billy's place and talked and prayed, without getting any indication he was hearing them at all. They kept up the daily visits, and finally their tenacity was rewarded. Billy agreed to come to church!

The news that Billy Blay was going to be in church amazed the public, and a larger-than-usual crowd came to the service that night, at least partly to see if Billy would really be there. Billy came, and everyone was astonished that he was not only sober, but clean-shaven as well, and dressed in reasonably clean clothes for the first time in anyone's memory. They could scarcely recognize him. Although Billy had not overtly responded to them, the ministers' visits to him the past several days had given him the resolve he needed to turn away from liquor and become a man again. When Brother Van led the exhortation that night for the repentant ones to "come to Jesus," Billy Blay was the first person to come forward.

After the service, while Will and Tom were talking with

him about the Christian life he had just committed himself to, Billy asked, "Would you please get me a pen and some paper? I must write a letter to my wife and children in Wisconsin." That the former sot could read and write was a revelation in itself; that he had a wife and family was a still greater surprise. Breaking a twelve-year alcoholic silence, he wrote the letter. While he awaited a reply, Billy put himself in the care of the two ministers, who found him to be a great help in their revival. Because of his long bout with alcoholism and his dramatic conversion, Billy was able to persuade a number of others to make the wonderful journey from darkness into light.

It was not long until he heard from his wife. She was in poor health, she said, but she was overjoyed at last to hear from her long-lost husband, and she asked him to come home to her and the children, who were by now quite fully grown. Billy had no money for such a trip, but the two places in town that knew him best, the church and the saloon, both took up collections for Billy and presented him more than enough money for the trip, with their best wishes. Billy returned home to a joyous family reunion, and became a missionary-preacher in the Wisconsin lumber camps.

The story of Billy Blay was an important lesson to Brother Van. They had been told that Billy was a hopeless case, but they saw a miracle take place in his life. To say that any person is hopeless is to imply that God is helpless. If Billy Blay's life could be transformed by the power of the gospel, anyone's life could be. After this, he felt full assurance when he entered a saloon to preach and sing, and to invite people to attend services. Nobody can fall so low that God cannot reach down and lift him up.

Shortly after the successful conclusion of the Virginia City revival, Will and Tom were en route to the Madison River school, which was to be the site of their next revival. To reach the school, they would have to ford the Madison River. It was spring, the river would be running full to its banks, and crossing it would be something of a challenge. Iliff was carrying a package for his wife from her family in the East which had been dropped off the stage in Iliff's care in Virginia City. He had no idea what was in it, but he knew it was important to keep it safe and sound.

Their small wagon rolled and bumped along the trail without mishap, and eventually they came to the river, so high that even the brush along the bank was standing in the water. Their small rig didn't seem to be adequate for the situation.

"What do you think, Will? Shall we give it up?"

"You know we can't do that, Tom. Those people are expecting us, and we can't disappoint them. I've never yet missed a meeting for any reason, and we can't start now."

"Well, then" said Iliff, "we'll just have to make it across, and right here looks to be as good a place as any. Can you swim, Will?"

"Not a stroke."

"Then you get up on the seat beside me. I'll drive the team, and you keep that package dry, no matter what."

It took some coaxing, but the horses finally agreed to plunge into the icy water. About halfway across, they came upon a sandbar under only about three feet of water, which gave them a chance to rest before undertaking the last half of the crossing. It proved to be a much deeper channel, and the horses had to swim while the carriage floated to the opposite shore. Brother Van carefully laid the package on the buggy seat before he jumped into the water to help Iliff and the horses get the rig up onto the bank. Several times they had it almost on the bank, when a horse or man would slip, and the buggy rolled back into the water. Finally, with a mighty lunge, they got the buggy up on the bank, and only then did

Iliff spot his wife's package bobbing in the current as it floated downstream.

Iliff cried excitedly, "The package! Will! Get the package!" as he gestured wildly in the direction of the brown lump on the water.

Forgetting for the moment that he couldn't swim, Will jumped into the water and struck out for the package. With much mighty splashing and floundering, he finally reached it and hauled it back to shore.

Both men were soaked to the skin for all their troubles, and they hadn't managed to keep the package dry, but it was not long until they began to see humor in the situation, and sat there on the riverbank, laughing like a couple of schoolboys. A rancher came by who had met them once before, and he invited them to come to his home to get dried out and have a hot meal before they made the rest of their journey. At the ranch house, they decided they had better open the very damp bundle for Mary Iliff. They found it contained a lovely silk dress, and when it was dried, they were thankful that it looked none the worse for its cold water washing in the Madison River.

The only actual loss in the incident was a bundle of Will's sermon notes which had gotten knocked overboard in the jostling along the far bank, which Brother Van jokingly declared had apparently been "too heavy to float."

There was no contest in deciding it had to be Brother Van who would preach at the memorial service in Missoula for Tom Iliff when he died in 1917. Because he loved the man so much, it was a very difficult assignment for Will. In the course of his sermon, Brother Van said,

> There is no friendship so lasting as Christian friendship,
> and especially that which grows out of activity
> along the frontier of the Rocky Mountain country,

where we would often take, as it were, our lives in our own hands, crossing rivers and mountain streams that were not bridged, and often going among the hostile Indians to hold the first Christian service in some mining camp or new frontier settlement. One of our favorite hymns was:

> My latest sun is sinking fast,
> My race is nearly run;
> My strongest trials now are past,
> My triumph is begun.

How we shall all miss thee! But heaven is nearer and Christ is dearer than ever before. May thy saintly mantle rest not only upon the family, but upon the whole church. Yes, to thee the gates of heaven have opened wide, and thou didst go sweeping through, all washed in Jesus' blood. . . .

One of Brother Van's favorite phrases was, "Workmen may fall but the work goes on." Iliff had been instrumental in the establishment of many important Methodist ventures, and the work would go on. He had built well, for the ages and not for the moment. But Will knew beyond doubt that one of the truly great workmen had fallen, and the church would not soon find another such as Thomas C. Iliff to carry its banners forward and hold aloft the torch of God's eternal truth.

Next to Tom Iliff, no doubt the most important man in Brother Van's life was his "excellent colleague," Francis Riggin. They were born in the same year, not too many miles distant from each other, and they began their careers together in Montana. In the Montana Methodist ministry, their lives ran a parallel course for more than 45 years.

After his service at Virginia City, Riggin was made presiding elder of the Butte District, with his main concern being to establish a church in the mining town that would one day be known as "the richest hill on earth." It would, in its heyday, be the largest town in Montana, but in the time Riggin went there, it boasted of only about 50 inhabitants. To get started in developing the new church, Riggin called upon Brother Van to assist him in a series of evangelistic services. They had worked together so amicably before, and had developed such a sure-fire approach to revivalism that Riggin didn't consider calling anyone except Brother Van. Brother Van would joke, years later, about preaching in Butte to a congregation that lacked only 10 of being the entire population of the city, meaning there had been 40 people present.

Riggin was a man not only of great ability, but of supreme dedication. Unlike other places where he had worked, Riggin found the residents in Butte were less than enthusiastic about rising to support the establishment of the Mountain View Methodist Church, so he himself put up the money to buy the lots in uptown Butte. He signed the note that would finance the construction of the building, which the trustees of the church had refused to sign. We don't know how Riggin happened to have the money, but it is true that during three years of work on the project, Riggin paid into the founding of the church twice as many dollars as the church paid him. His persistence paid off. Mountain View church was established and is still rendering service, more than a hundred years later.

Brother Van and Riggin were again put together on important new work for the years 1887-1889, when they were assigned to the Fort Benton-Great Falls circuit. Fort Benton was the established church, while Great Falls was to be the new development. To go the forty miles from Fort Benton to Great Falls, they had to ride horses or drive a horse and buggy, and then rent a hotel room in Great Falls; there was not yet any church or parsonage. Their expenses were exactly double what their income was from offerings received at Great Falls services. Riggin told of a time when he and two visiting pastors had to sleep in the same three-quarter size bed in Great Falls, and pay a dollar apiece for the privilege.

Later, a Mrs. Cunningham provided free room and board for them when they were in town, which helped the ministers very much. The church took root quickly in Great Falls, and Riggin soon took up residence there so he could look after the work more closely.

Brother Van was stricken in the winter of 1888 with an illness so severe that it nearly took his life, but details are lacking to indicate exactly what he had contracted. It was widely believed to have been tick fever, and it may indeed have been, but that seems a very strange malady for a person to get in the winter. It seems more logical to assume it must have been some type of pneumonia, no doubt aggravated by the fact that Brother Van kept going when he was ill, until he finally became so ill he simply could not keep going. Whatever it was, it was nearly fatal, and it took him the greater part of a year to recover. No doubt one of the things that helped his recovery was Ida Riggin's good cooking and tender care.

Many of the supporting facts are missing, but at one point during his recuperation, Brother Van was sent to Seattle for convalescence, perhaps in the thought that the low altitude and the fresh sea air would be beneficial for him. Some recuperation! The records show that he conducted a revival for a local Methodist Church in Seattle. His holidays were almost always working holidays, and it turns out his convalescence was also a working one. Presumably, like everyone else, Brother Van had occasional colds or bouts with influenza, but this is the only illness, prior to his final illness, that he ever suffered that was serious enough to actually disrupt his work.

In making his annual conference report at the end of their first year, Riggin wrote, "Brother Van and I have had many a siege together, but never more sweetly and triumphantly than this year. And though we have both had perhaps the severest trials of our endurance and our faith, we have never had clearer faith nor grander hopes, nor sweeter association with God and his people."

It is a tribute to the two men's character and to the quality of their personal relationship that they worked together so closely for so many years and remained firm in their friendship. Of course there had to have been occasional disagreements and misunderstandings, but there is no record of any serious or long-standing problems between them. One slight problem arose when the second Methodist Church built in Great Falls was named Van Orsdel Methodist Church, in honor of Brother Van, who was at that time the District Superintendent. Riggin felt it was unfair to name the church in honor of Brother Van, when he had played an even larger role than Brother Van in establishing the church. It made no lasting difference to Riggin, however, and the name was changed, not many years later, to First Methodist.

Chapter Seven

...

*I*n his youthful dreams about coming west, Will had perceived himself as a missionary to the Indians. Before he made the voyage up the Missouri River, though, he had a clearer vision of what his life's work would be. He was going out West, as he told the steamship captain, "to sing and preach and encourage the people to be good," and for forty-seven years that is exactly what he did. But the welfare of Native American souls was always one of his greatest concerns, and he cherished every opportunity that came his way to bring the gospel to the Indians and to associate with them.

Brother Van's first opportunity to minister to the Indians came just a few months after he arrived in Montana. Before he had ever gone to Helena, he had already been to the Blackfeet and Piegan Indian Agency where he became acquainted with some of the key people. They invited him to come to the reservation any time he could and told him he would be more than welcome to meet the people and hold religious services for any who were interested.

He found such an opportunity in the winter of 1873, during a period of time when the weather had turned fairly warm and there seemed to be little threat of snow. He rode his horse Jonathan from Helena to Choteau, and consulted again with the people at the Indian agency about going to the Indians and holding some religious services. They not only agreed to let him do this, but also provided an interpreter to accompany him. The Indians knew little or no English, and Brother Van didn't speak the Indian language at all, so an interpreter would be essential if there was to be any communication between them.

So Brother Van, accompanied by his interpreter, rode off to find the Indians. Before long, they came upon nearly two thousand Blackfeet camped a few miles east of the Teton River, in a place known as "Freeze-out Flats." Riding into their camp on a Sunday afternoon, he told his interpreter to pass the word that he would hold worship services that evening. When evening came, a large number of the natives gathered in the largest tent, and the service began, with Brother Van speaking through his interpreter. The hour was about half over when an Indian brave stuck his head through the tent flap and spoke excitedly for a few seconds about something. Upon his words, all the Indian braves immediately arose and left the service.

Bewildered by this turn of events, Will hoped he had not said or done anything that caused offense and was relieved to learn from his interpreter that it was nothing like that. He said the message-bearer had informed the worshipers that a band of marauding Indians had managed to sneak into the Blackfeet corral and had driven off 40 or 50 of their best horses. The horses in the corrals were used for buffalo hunting and for guarding the camp, and without them the Blackfeet were pretty much afoot.

Without hesitation, Will said, "Tell them to take our horses and see if they can catch up with the thieves." This they did, and after about two hours they returned, driving ahead of them the horses they had recaptured from their enemies. Then, to a man, they trooped back into the tent and demanded that the worship service be continued. Little Plume, the young chieftain of the tribe, was grateful for the assistance of the two white men in recapturing their horses, and in token of that appreciation, he invited the minister to go with them on a buffalo hunt the next morning.

Leaving the Indian encampment before daybreak, the hunting party had to ride about eight miles before they came upon a herd of buffalo. They stayed in ravines and other low-lying areas in order to avoid being seen on the open plains by the buffalo. When they came upon the herd, grazing peacefully or resting on a ridge several hundred yards away, the hunters knew they had not yet done anything to alarm them. Buffalo, when frightened, were known to stampede, rushing headlong at a full gallop, demolishing everything in their path. The Indians often used this to their advantage by forcing the buffalo to stampede in the direction of a cliff, called a "buffalo jump," over which they would fall to their death. Other Indians waited at the bottom of the cliff to kill any that had survived the fall. Then followed the huge task of butchering all those thousands of pounds of meat and preparing the hides for numerous future uses.

Here, there was no cliff over which to drive them, so Little Plume stationed his warriors at several points along a ravine that led down from the hill where the buffalo grazed. He sent another group of riders to encircle the herd and come up behind them, forcing them down the hill toward the waiting hunters. The prime feat of such a chase was to kill the "king buffalo," the leader of the herd, which was always an especially large male. The monarch was thought to have better leather in his hide, and it was considered a feather in one's bonnet to be the one to drop the king. Since this hunt was in Brother Van's honor, he was accorded the privilege of killing the king buffalo.

Brother Van didn't dare to let the Indians know it, but he

was literally quaking in his boots. He had not hunted before, and had some doubts about his ability to kill the king buffalo. When the herd came thundering off the hill, he waited tensely on his horse until the chief pointed out which one was the king, and signaled him to go and shoot it. Praying he would be able to succeed, Brother Van spurred Jonathan into full pursuit of the monstrous beast which had just sped by. The other hunters, meanwhile, were killing some buffalo, but the sound of gunshots could scarcely be heard above the thunder of the buffalo hooves. Jonathan was a strong runner, and quickly drew abreast of the magnificent leader of the herd. With a great deal more luck than skill, Brother Van cocked his revolver and fired. The great bull was dead before he hit the ground, shot cleanly in the head. The kill was as neat as could be done and won for Brother Van the great admiration of the Blackfeet.

In later years whenever Brother Van had a chance to retell the story of the buffalo hunt, he added, "that buffalo was killed by prayer." He was a very skillful and experienced rider but not at all acquainted with firearms. Yet he knew it was very important for him to make good on the hunt. If he had missed, some of the braves who were watching would have taken over and killed the king buffalo, but their help wasn't needed, as it turned out. He was praying hard that his shot would be true, and it was.

The event was immortalized by the famous Montana cowboy artist, Charles M. Russell, in his painting called "Brother Van Shooting Buffalo." The tribe later expressed its appreciation for Brother Van's courage and marksmanship and for his spiritual leadership so generously and lovingly given by making him an honorary chief and presenting him with a long, feathered headdress emblematic of his high rank in the tribe. His name in the tribe was "Great-Heart."

At the rate buffalo were being killed by the white men,

Brother Van was afraid that the Indians were in danger of losing the way of life that had made them a proud and successful race for thousands of years. Buffalo were the staff of life to the Indians, and when Will had first come to Montana they were more than abundant. Topping a rise where the land spread out in panoramic vistas, a rider could sometimes see huge herds of them in several directions, with hundreds of animals in each herd. Stories abound of how great herds of the shaggy monsters, in crossing the Missouri, would force a steamship to hold up for fully half a day, and how the solid wall of their bodies would actually cause the water on the upstream side to rise two feet or more, while on the downstream side the water level would drop. Charles M. Russell depicted exactly such a scene on a birthday greeting letter that he wrote to Brother Van.

The Indian way of living and hunting had preserved and maintained the number of buffalo for untold generations. The white man's wasteful and outrageous ways would surely mean the end of the species before long. But Brother Van's interest in ministering to the Indians was not born of sympathy for them; he genuinely loved the Indians and they loved him. In reading in his journals one finds that on those occasions where he tells of having held services with an Indian group, he invariably added a remark such as "God bless their dear souls."

His concern for the Indians' souls was deep and genuine. In dealing with the white people, there were many first-time conversions, but much of the time his work involved calling people back to a faith from which they had drifted away. In the case of the Indians, he believed himself to be dealing with pagans, people who had never been acquainted with Christianity, to whom he was introducing Christ for the first time. It was for that reason that he had such a special affection and concern for the Indian people and desired so greatly

170

Brother Van, whom the Blackfeet Indians made an honorary chieftain and named "Great-Heart," loved to be in Browning for Fourth of July celebrations.

to do missionary work among them whenever he could.

Brother Van spent Easter of 1894 with the Indians at the Epworth Piegan Indian Mission west of Sun River, a center of missionary work among the Indians which he had been instrumental in establishing in conjunction with the government school for Indians located there. Like the rest of his work, this mission was started under his leadership. But as soon as possible, a regular minister was assigned to remain there and maintain the operation, while Brother Van went on to other places. This was particularly necessary in the case of the work with Indians, because his regular assignments were always in parishes that principally served the white communities. But if there was an Indian settlement in the vicinity, Brother Van could be counted on to go there, to preach and pray and sing, and perhaps to get something organized that would be a permanent religious establishment.

Easter Sunday morning he attended the Sabbath school at the Government Indian School, and in the afternoon there was a regular church service with about 20 whites and more than 100 Indians worshiping together. The Reverend E. S. Dutcher was the new pastor of the mission, and he and Brother Van spoke to the Indians with the aid of two interpreters. In his journal, Brother Van wrote:

> I never saw greater interest in a congregation on the subject of religion. Fourteen Indian children where baptized. . . .our hearts burned as we took the Lord's Super, the first in this new mission, and the first ever administered by a Protestant on this reservation. Then came the first missionary collection among those pagan Piegan Indians, $36.75. A number of Indian boys and girls giving from 5 to 50 cts. Bishop Foss Dutcher, born the day the Epworth League was born, give his first missionary collection - two cents.
>
> This has been a glorious day. His love fills all our souls tonight. O such sweet glorious peace. God is in this work and great good will come of it. Many bright converts. Prais God from whom all blessings flow.

In his later years, Brother Van made it a point as often as possible to be at Browning over the Fourth of July, to celebrate America's independence with the Native Americans of the Blackfeet tribe. He had been formally adopted into the tribe as an honorary chief, and with the position came an enormous and colorful chief's headband to wear on ceremonial occasions. Brother Van purely loved to be at the head of the grand Fourth of July parade, riding his pony and proudly wearing his band of plumage.

When he could be present, Brother Van was almost always given the honor of delivering the main address of the day, in which he took the greatest delight. Fervently patriotic, he was never better in oratory than when had the freedom to interweave love of God and love of country into a single speech.

The Great Falls *Daily Tribune* on July 7, 1918, reported on the Fourth of July activities at Browning in which more than 3000 people participated (which was far more than just the local population):

> ....The orator of the day was Brother Van, and being at his best, the occasion and place to his liking, he covered himself with new honors and during his speech he held up the American flag like a mighty general leading his comrades on to certain victory. The applause that greeted him at the close must have cheered his heart....

When word of Brother Van's death came to the reservation, one of the Blackfeet Indian men said, "So Brother Van is dead. Now the Indian has a friend in heaven."

Not very many white men have ever been made honorary chiefs, and not very many have so sincerely and earnestly cared about the Indian people and the welfare of their souls.

Chapter Eight

• • •

The lives of legendary characters
soon become surrounded by myths. Myths have a way of
taking on a life of their own, and truth often must take a
back seat. They are such good stories that their lack of
veracity doesn't seem to bother a lot of people. One such
myth that will not die insists that Brother Van, on arriving at
Fort Benton, preached his first sermon in Montana in a
saloon. The account of his arrival exists in his own words,
and Brother Van assuredly did not preach in a saloon that
day. People refuse to accept Brother Van's own explanation
of what he did, probably because the untruth seems so much
more exciting. It is true that he preached in saloons a great
many other times, though. In all his life, he never touched a
drop of liquor, but he was always on good terms with
saloon-keepers and their patrons, and was very much at ease
being in a saloon. His uncompromising honesty won the
respect of even the most hardened frontiersmen, who
accepted him wherever they met him, including the saloons.

Brother Van knew the importance of making a good first
impression. Being neat and well-dressed was one of his
trademarks, and it was not always easy, in primitive conditions, to maintain a neat and clean appearance. In his black
broadcloth suit, long-tailed coat, white "biled" shirt, necktie

and black broad-brimmed hat, he made a sharp contrast to the usual visitor to a saloon. Conversation would stop, and all eyes would be on him when he entered. There were usually people present who knew him, and they would greet him warmly. If nobody knew him, he would introduce himself. Occasionally some rowdy would try to badger him, but such persons always came out second-best in an exchange with Brother Van.

Brother Van rarely just came into town and headed for the nearest saloon, intent on preaching there. But sometimes he needed to go to the saloon to find a person, or to get some information or directions. If events naturally led him to a saloon, he didn't back away. He knew he would always be welcome to hold services on a moment's notice, but he preferred to have more conventional settings when they were available. He rode into Philbrook one Sunday afternoon, having preached that morning in Utica. A leather bag hooked over the saddle horn carried his extra clothing, while the regular saddle bags contained his Bible and song books. Brother Van traveled light. Having been invited on his previous trip to stay the night with the Morrisons, he made his way there. Supper was in the making, but Mrs. Morrison said he had time to go to the hall where church services would be held, and get it arranged as he wanted it. He expected it would be necessary, as it often was in other places he preached, to clear away the empty whiskey bottles and air the place out a little.

On the way from Morrison's house to the meeting hall, he had to walk past Charlie Tarkett's saloon. Tarkett had been a cowboy in Texas, and was reputed to have killed at least three men. It was rumored, and was probably true, that he had left Texas by popular demand, leaving no forwarding address. Reflecting the character of its owner, his bar was a hangout for some of the frontier's most undesirable characters.

A few men lounged outside the saloon, smoking and talking, and one of them recognized Brother Van as he passed. Stopping to talk with them a minute, he was introduced to those he didn't know. One of them, wanting to give the parson a bad time, said, "Come on in, Brother Van, and I'll buy you a drink."

He wasn't prepared for the preacher's prompt acceptance. "Sounds good to me, Tom. I'm pretty dry after riding over from Utica." With all the others following closely, Brother Van and his new acquaintance went inside and up to the bar. The bartender began taking orders for drinks, and when he came to Brother Van, the minister said, "I'd like an orange drink, please." He drank it while visiting comfortably with the men around him.

"Well, I'd better be going. I've got to clean up the hall before church tonight," Will said as he finished his drink.

"Wait, Brother Van," one of the patrons called out, "Sing us a song before you go."

Quickly surveying the aggregation of men, Brother Van tried to think what song would be most fitting, and decided he would sing "Where is My Wandering Boy Tonight?" Without accompaniment, he sang in a strong, clear voice:

O where is my wandering boy tonight,
The boy of my tenderest care?
The boy who was once my joy and light,
The child of my love and prayer.
O where is my boy tonight?
O where is my boy tonight?
My heart overflows,
For I love him, he knows;
O where is my boy tonight?

Though steel-blue revolvers hung menacingly at their hips,

tears brimmed in their eyes, as the range-hardened men thought of home and mother. And then he preached the kind of sermon he usually gave in saloons, not one dealing with a Bible text, but dealing with the men's hearts. He spoke to the men in the bar, saying, "Now don't forget your ma and pa. There is a light shining in their window for you. If you can't go back and see them, at least write them a letter. Do it tonight before you go to bed."

He could tell he had gotten their interest, so he continued, "Your ma and pa are getting old, and you may not see them again while they live. But you can decide to live in such a way that you'll meet them in heaven."

And then he began another song:

Tell mother I'll be there
In answer to her prayer;
This message to her, angels, sweetly bear.
Tell mother I'll be there
Heaven's joys with her to share,
O tell my darling mother I'll be there.

Ending the second song, Brother Van spoke into the greatest silence ever known in that "round the clock" establishment. "Fellows, I've got to be going or I'll be late for supper. I visited you in your gathering place, and now I'd like for you to visit God's place and mine tonight at eight o'clock." Waving his arm in a general salute to everyone, he left.

At ten minutes to eight, Charlie Tarkett stunned the crowd by announcing in a loud voice, "Finish up your drinks in a hurry, men. Bar's closed for an hour, and we're all going to go hear Brother Van preach." To a man, they went, and they listened respectfully. The room was packed, because people from all around had known for weeks that Brother Van would be preaching that night, and they wouldn't miss it for anything. When the service was over, the men from Charlie Tarkett's saloon were not even eager to get back to their drinking. They had caught a glimpse of something much finer they could do with their lives. Shaking hands with them after the service, Brother Van thought to himself, "There's nothing so tough and dangerous about these boys. They're just misguided, and need Jesus to straighten them out."

Brother Van met people on their terms, but dealt with them on his terms. Rather than descending to their level, he lifted them up to his level, and was never the least bit patronizing or condescending toward them. He saw and admired their good qualities, but he always kept in mind that he was God's ambassador, and he never failed to ask them in the name of Jesus to come to higher ground. Frontier people could spot a phony a long way off and held such persons in contempt. Nobody ever thought Brother Van was phony.

In later life, Will was a good friend of Charles M. Russell, the noted artist. Although Russell was a good man, he was not a churchman, as many of Brother Van's friends were not. The two first met in 1884, when Russell was a youth of 16 and Will was 36.

High up in the Judith Basin is a lesser region known as "Pig Eye Basin." Russell was living there with an older man named Jake Hoover, and the two made their living by trapping animals and selling furs, and by shooting game which they sold for meat for the tables of the ranchers in the area. Returning one day at dusk from a hunting trip, their horses heavily loaded with fresh deer and elk meat, they decided to put up for the night at the Babcock ranch. "Old Bab," as Babcock was called, was a typical mountain man, as rough and tough as the mountains he loved, but "all heart from the belt up," as Russell put it. Because of his boundless capacity for friendliness, Old Bab's place was the favorite stopping point in the whole area for assorted bullwhackers, hunters, cowboys, prospectors and drifters.

Kid Russell and Jake Hoover weren't the first ones this evening to avail themselves of Old Bab's hospitality; inside the cabin they found an assortment of wayfarers who had arrived ahead of them. Russell and Hoover had no more than gotten inside when yet another rider approached. As the figure emerged in the gathering dark, the distinctive cut of his clothing announced his identity. Before he could possibly make out the man's face, Old Bab was shouting a greeting: "Welcome, Brother Van! Real glad to see you." It happened that Kid Russell was the only one present whom Brother Van had not met before somewhere, so all of them responded to his arrival with a variety of friendly greetings. Introducing the youngster, Old Bab said, "Brother Van, this here's Kid Russell. He's doin' some hunting and trapping with Jake Hoover."

While Will was exchanging news with the others, Old Bab took Russell aside and told him, "Boy, I don't savvy many psalm-singers, but Brother Van deals square."

By the dim light of a bacon-grease lamp, the men were soon seated around Old Bab's table, enjoying a wonderful meal of elk steak compliments of Russell and Hoover, boiled beans, bread, coffee, and dried apples. Some of the men were "tough customers" with notches in their guns, and most of them had not heard or said a prayer in years, but before the meal, Old Bab asked Brother Van to offer a prayer of thanks. At the end of his prayer, someone echoed the preacher's "Amen." Years later, in a letter to Brother Van, Russell spoke of that event:

"I am not sure (who said the 'Amen' after the prayer) but I think it was the man I heard later was or had been a road agent. I was sixteen years old then, Brother Van, but I have never forgotten your stay at Old Bab's with men whose talk was generally emphasized with fancy profanity; but while you were with us, although they had to talk slow and careful, there was never a slip. The outlaw at Bab's was a sinner, and none of us were saints, but our hearts were clean at least while you gave thanks, and the holdup said 'Amen'."

W. T. Cowan of Box Elder said, "It was one of the joys of my life to see Brother Van meet the various characters who usually hang out around a frontier store and post office. When he came into town, his greeting, in his usual cheery way, was 'How!' or 'How goes it, brother?' Men whom I knew to be anything but angels were touched by his great soul, and I never heard a slurring remark about him in a group after he had greeted them and departed."

On July 19, 1894, Brother Van rode the train about 40 miles from Havre eastward to Harlem, two towns which are nestled about 50 miles below the Canadian border, and from Harlem he took the stagecoach south 60 miles to the gold-mining camp of Landusky in the Little Rocky Mountains. The Reigel family operated a sawmill not far from Landusky, and Will asked the stage driver to let him off when they got there. He'd met the Reigels before on several occasions, but had not yet been to their home. They were overjoyed to see him when he arrived and insisted on having him be their guest for as long as he would be in the area, as he had hoped they would. The 46-year-old preacher appreciated the fine Christian family and was not oblivious to the fact that they had a very delightful unmarried daughter whom they called Miss Leafy.

For the record, perhaps it should be noted here that for more than 25 years, Brother Van and Miss Leafy were to maintain a somewhat serious relationship. She often served as his secretary, and she would have married him in a minute, but Brother Van had long ago decided to remain unmarried. In a letter to him, Leafy once wrote the words "I love you," and there were in many of her letters veiled references to the hugging and kissing that he liked so well. Those who knew Miss Leafy said that she was "one in a million," and it is a pity that Brother Van never saw fit to take her into his life completely.

Brother Van saw to it that word was sent around the community that he would hold preaching services at the Reigel sawmill the next night, which would be Saturday, and there would be church services in the town of Landusky, Sunday morning at eleven. Landusky's residents couldn't believe the news. It was astonishing enough to think of a service at the Reigel mill, but to consider holding a service in Landusky was preposterous! Speculation ran high as to which of the town's ruffians would break up the meeting with his revolver, but there were so many candidates they couldn't make a choice. God's name was only heard in Landusky in profane oaths. Besides, where would he hold a service? There wasn't even a school, much less a church, and every shanty in town was occupied. It would be interesting to see what the Reverend Mr. Van Orsdel would do now.

To everyone's surprise, over 35 people came to the service Saturday night at the Reigel mill, as Brother Van preached from Matthew 22:42 on the topic "What Think You of Christ?" The answer, for most of them, was that they had thought nothing of him, at least not in a very long time. His sermon reminded them there was another dimension to life that deserved consideration, the dimension of the spirit. Following the service, there was much friendly visiting, and some people expressed their concern about how he would hold a service on Sunday, now just hours away. In his usual air of unbridled optimism, he assured them he would find a place, or would preach in the street if he had to, but Landusky would have a Sunday church service.

The July Sunday morning dawned bright and clear. It was the glorious kind of day one finds in few places on earth outside Montana. The high-country elevation does not permit it to get too hot, and the cool mountain air is so refreshingly sweet that it is joyous just to stand in the sunshine and inhale great, deep breaths of it. In honor of this special occasion, the sawmill's lumber wagon had been cleaned and its wheels greased. The logging team which pulled it, accustomed to pine trees, bark and dust, had been carefully curried and brushed, and their harnesses gleamed in the sun with fresh oil. Brother Van's appearance in Landusky was going to be something special! Mrs. Reigel and Miss Leafy had taken extra care in pressing Brother Van's black suit and white shirt, to make him look princely as he came to town.

Seeming to sense the importance of the occasion, the team fairly pranced the three miles into town, and suddenly the wagon was at the north end of the town's main, and only, street. Spectators filled every doorway, and other faces were behind every curtained window, peering out at the sight of Brother Van, sitting erect and proud beside the driver, with a Bible in his lap.

The wagon rolled to a stop in front of the "Jew-Jake Saloon," which had just recently gone out of business, for unknown reasons. As soon as he saw it, Will knew it was the place for the service. It was just perfect, or would be with a little tidying up. While Mr. Reigel went to find Jew Jake and get his permission to use the place, Brother Van, Miss Leafy and Mrs. Reigel went in and gathered up the empty bottles that stood here and there, taking it on faith that they would be given permission. Magically, they found some empty boxes and some boards, and these were immediately transformed into benches. In minutes, the room that had been the hangout of drunks, rowdies and rustlers was well-filled with those who waited for the church service to begin. More than 75 people came, and a preacher never had a more peculiar congregation.

To earn its reputation as the most wicked mining town in all Montana, Landusky had to have some pretty unsavory characters. It did, indeed, and they were all in church that Sunday morning. Pike Landusky and Jew Jake, the town's two saloon proprietors, were there. Jew Jake, in a charitable mood, had agreed to let them use his abandoned saloon building, but he was widely noted for having both a peg leg and a bad temper, with a disposition to shoot anyone who strongly disagreed with him. On the front bench sat Johnny "Kid" Curry, one shirt sleeve hanging empty at his side. Beside him sat his brother Lonnie, and their partner in crime, Jim Thornhill. "Old Dad," a lumberjack who worked for Mr. Reigel, had taken a shine to Brother Van at the sawmill on Saturday evening, but had gone into town afterward and spent the whole night drinking, as was his custom, and was now roaring drunk. He did seem to know he was in church, though, because from where he sat on the floor in the back of the room, he would punctuate Brother Van's sermon at the most unlikely moments with shouts of "Hallelujah!" and "Amen!"

Will's sermon text was Matthew 6:10, "Thy kingdom come, thy will be done on earth as it is in heaven." As had been the case with the sermon at the sawmill, this one presented the people with something to think about that had not been on their minds for a long time. They knew all about imposing their will on others. In their desperate lives, the man who could draw his gun the fastest was the one who was right. But that reign of law was good only until someone came along who could draw still faster, and one always did, sooner or later. Now here was a man telling them there is a

*Families living in sod shanties on the Montana plains
offered their best hospitality when
Brother Van came to call.*

law that stands above all others, and can never be overruled. He told them that the reign of God in heaven could be brought to earth if people cared enough. It was a hopeful thought to desperate men; even to "Kid" Curry, who knew that he was going to die on the day that somebody rode into town who was faster on the draw.

Punctuated here and there by song, as well as by "Old Dad's" cries of "Amen!" the service came to the final part in which people were challenged to stand and declare their allegiance to that heavenly kingdom. Several stood for prayer, indicating their response, and nearly two hours had elapsed by the time the service was over. It had seemed only a short while, especially to "Old Dad," who had finally fallen into an alcoholic slumber on the floor.

Thirty-five children and adults came to the "church" again

that afternoon, and a Sunday school was officially organized, with Mr. Reigel as the superintendent. Now there would be weekly Christian instruction for the growing youngsters as well as for the adults. Brother Van preached in the Jew-Jake Saloon again that evening. When he left on the northbound stage to catch the train at Harlem, the people of Landusky were urgent in their requests for him to return soon.

This account of the first service in Landusky was written by Miss Leafy, who was there. Brother Van, in his journal for that date, made the customary modest remark and left out all the interesting details. He simply wrote of it: "God was present. I had great liberty."

Opportunities to minister to the rougher element of frontier life seemed to come looking for Brother Van—like the time he helped Keen Wyatt get his wagon train out of the mud.

Driving several yokes of oxen was no job for a boy or a weak man. A "bullwhacker" needed to have a superb vocabulary of profanity, for the common belief was that if one could not let out with some choice oaths as he laid on the whip, he wouldn't be able to get the oxen to budge. And if he couldn't drive the oxen, he would find himself working on the chuck wagon, a fate considerably worse than death to a cowboy. One of the most profane and most accomplished of all bullwhackers was Keen Wyatt, who drove freight from Fort Benton to Helena. It was claimed he could turn a wagon train with 22 yoke of oxen on a town's main street and not touch anything on either side.

But on one occasion, his luck ran out. Recent rains had softened the sod so that the weight of the cargo made the thin steel-rimmed wheels cut through the surface and sink deep into the wet gumbo. Brother Van was passing by, on his way to the bedside of a friend who was near death, but as he came upon the mired freight train, he called out, "Can I help you?"

Noting the characteristic garb the preacher wore, Keen Wyatt said, "You sure can, if you're not too stuck up."

Telling the man he was going on a sick call, Brother Van said, "A little mud is nothing to me, and I'll be glad to do what I can to help you get loose and on your way. How can I help?"

Wyatt gave him a club and placed him alongside a huge black ox that wasn't really trying to pull, now that the wagon was stuck. "Now," Keen said, "while I whip up the rest of them, you keep working on this black. Just whale the eternal __ __ __ out of him and get him to start pulling."

Nodding his understanding, Will took up his assigned post. Keen's whip, over 20 feet long, screamed through the air and landed on the backs of the straining beasts, accompanied by as choice a selection of foul oaths as Brother Van had ever heard. "Lean into the yoke, you lazy __ __ __ mongrels," Wyatt bellowed as he swung the whip with unerring accuracy.

"Praise God!" shouted Brother Van, energetically jabbing his stick in the black ox's ribs.

Their combined efforts goaded the oxen into pulling, and soon the wagons were free of the muck and on more solid ground. Climbing off the lead wagon, Wyatt pulled off his gloves and wiped his brow with his large red bandanna. Stepping up to Brother Van, he said, "That was a good piece of work. Let's shake on it. You're the best __ __ __ preacher I ever saw!"

The frontier in Montana was slow to vanish, and Brother Van was constantly alert to find places where the gospel had not yet been preached. One such opportunity came to him in 1909. About 30 miles northwest of Great Falls, on the Great Northern Railway's branch line from Great Falls to Shelby, lies the tiny hamlet of Collins. It consisted of the railroad station, two saloons, one store, one hotel, and a number of hastily-erected shacks in which the few residents lived. On one of his trips between Great Falls and Shelby, when the train stopped for a short while at Collins, Brother Van met the Collins station agent, E. J. Liptak. Mr. Liptak told him that nobody had ever held services in Collins, and a lot of the old-timers there, who had heard him at other places over the years, were most anxious for Brother Van to come to Collins and hold a service in that newly-established community.

Ever anxious to score yet another "first," Brother Van accepted the offer at once. Consulting his date book, he found a Sunday not far in the future that was still open, and agreed with Mr. Liptak to be there. Liptak said he would publicize the date widely and would arrange to have the meeting at the community's one-room school.

Gambling and drinking were about the only diversions the town of Collins normally provided its residents, and most were happy enough to have it so. Realizing the threat the saloons posed to the success of the coming church service, Liptak saw that a petition was circulated, asking that the saloons close their doors during the hour reserved for the service, and it was unanimously agreed upon. Further, it was agreed that every person in town must attend church, no matter how much carousing and drinking he had done on Saturday night.

The big day finally came, and Brother Van arrived, looking regal, as he always did, in his best preaching garb. The entire town of Collins turned out for the service—all 25 or 30 of them. At the appropriate time in the service, Mr. Liptak literally "took" the offering. As he passed his Stetson hat, any person who dropped in a small coin was glowered at until he dug deeper. The total collection came to $45.50, an average of $1.50 for every man, woman and child present.

As the service continued, an old sheepherder who had spent the previous night and day drinking and was still more

than a little "under the influence," insisted on having Brother
Van sing "Diamonds in the Rough." So loud and persistent
was he that Will had no choice but to sing in order to quiet
him. Others then began placing requests, and Brother Van
managed only to squeeze in bits of his sermon between the
songs. Here, as always, the song most often and loudly called
for was "Harvest Time," also often called "Over and Over."
Brother Van sang it thousands of times, over the years,
always with feeling, for its words never failed to remind him
of his own life and his calling as a minister on Montana's
frontier. Written by the Reverend W. A. Spencer, D.D., in
Montana it is known as "Brother Van's Song," even by those
who have never heard of "Harvest Time." So, in response to
numerous requests, Brother Van stood before the whole town
of Collins and sang:

> The seed I have scattered in springtime with weeping,
> And watered with tears and with dews from on high;
> Another may shout when the harvesters, reaping,
> Shall gather my grain in the sweet by and by.
>
> Chorus:
> Over and over, yes, deeper and deeper,
> My heart is pierced through with life's sorrowing cry;
> But the tears of the sower and the songs of the reaper
> Shall mingle together in joy, by and by.
>   By and by, by and by,
>   By and by, by and by,
> Yes, the tears of the sower and the songs of the reaper
> Shall mingle together in joy, by and by.
>
> Another may reap what in springtime I've planted,
> Another rejoice in the fruit of my pain;
> Not knowing my tears when in summer I fainted
> While toiling, sad-hearted, in sunshine and rain.

188

Chorus

The thorns will have choked and the summer sun
    blasted
The most of the seed which in springtime I've sown,
But the Lord who has watched while my weary toil
lasted
Will give me a harvest for what I have done.

Chorus

After the final verse and chorus, a doxology was
added:

Then palms of victory, crowns of glory,
Palms of victory I shall wear.

Today, in the United Methodist Churches of Montana, the regular hymnal of the national denomination is used. But do not be surprised to find pasted inside the front or back cover the words and music to "Harvest Time," Brother Van's song.

A church service such as the one in Collins was typically Montana and typically Brother Van. Neither one stood much on formalities. Montanans were kind, decent and mannerly folk, but weren't long on refinement. But they all knew when someone was on the level, and they all knew Brother Van always was. They were indeed diamonds in the rough, and Brother Van polished them a little at every opportunity.

When he went to the far northeastern Montana community of Scobey in 1913 to pay a visit as the district superintendent, he assisted them in getting the church's building program under way. The local pastor was a little meek in his fund-raising efforts, but Brother Van took him by the arm and said, "Come on, brother, we're working for the Lord!" From one end of the town's one main street to the other, they stopped at every place of business, asking for donations to help build the Methodist Church. The pastor was reluctant to ask the saloons to contribute, but Brother Van insisted, "Let's go in, brother. We need the money!"

Liberal donations were received. Each saloon-keeper gave one hundred dollars, a sizable sum for those days, and they gave it gladly, knowing that Brother Van never represented an unworthy cause, and never misrepresented any cause. Even saloon-keepers, Will said, would not want to raise their children in a town that had no churches. Without the least hesitation, Will would walk into a saloon and ask the bartender for money, just as if he were the most devoted follower of the church. It was an approach that never failed to work.

On one occasion when Brother Van needed some money for a cause, one of his "diamond in the rough" friends engaged in a poker game in a local saloon pledging that his winnings, if any, would all go to Brother Van. Great interest focused on that gaming table as the unorthodox fund-raising project got under way. The fellow's luck happened to be unusually good that night, and he soon had a substantial sum in winnings, and he immediately went to find Brother Van and presented him the money. There was a lot of speculation that the minister would not accept such "tainted money" as a gift, but Brother Van was glad to take it, saying, "I accept the gift, with gratitude. The devil has had control of this money long enough; it's time it worked for the Lord awhile."

This was not just a bit of unorthodox policy that happened to work; it really made sense to Brother Van. Why shouldn't the saloons support the church? If it is a good and proper thing for anyone else to give to the Lord's work, why wouldn't that also apply to saloon-keepers? It made a lot of sense to him to transfer all the funds he could from the devil's ledger to the Lord's. Raising money was not an end in itself to Brother Van; it was also a means of evangelism. When a saloon-keeper gave money to help build a church, there was some possibility of getting him to focus on the welfare of the church, and the door was at least partly open to win the man to Christ.

Despite what some considered moral laxity in dealing with the saloon crowd, Brother Van was sometimes criticized for his unbending convictions about certain things. He took the Sabbath very seriously, and many activities were prohibited on the Sabbath. He refused to ride trains on Sunday and thereby require someone to be at work on his behalf. While visiting in Minneapolis, he and Francis Riggin walked 12 miles on a Sunday because they refused to ride the streetcar. He would not even write letters on Sunday, except to Jennie, who was a very special case. He declined to officiate at the funeral of a very dear friend, because to do so would have required that he take the train on Sunday from Great Falls.

He was known to expel people from church for conduct unbecoming a Christian. This included drinking alcohol and taking part in public dances. His strict moral code was not for laymen only; the ministers who worked under him had to be above reproach in their lives also.

Like any great person, Brother Van had some detractors. Some were jealous of his great popularity and enormous influence, and some were critical of his way of doing certain things. Mr. E. R. Russell was Brother Van's secretary when he was in Fort Benton. Russell was the stenographer for the county court and had a special flair for writing, so he was a fine choice as a secretary. He loved and respected Brother Van, but could see his human foibles more clearly than most.

When Brother Van ate at the Russell home, Mrs. Russell seated him at the back corner of the dining table, where he couldn't get up until everyone else did. She had learned that if he was seated anywhere out in the open, he would gulp his food and be up before anyone else was half done, pacing the floor and chafing to get at his dictation.

Russell also said, in a letter to a friend, with reference to Brother Van, "...we have great difficulty putting up with some of his mannerisms, particularly at the table. Do you remember how he sucked his soup? Well, he is as bad as ever, and we sometimes think worse."

Russell makes the amusing comment, "Rev. W. W. Van Orsdel has secretaries from one end of the land to the other, each one the best that ever was. I don't see how the old fellow can keep his self-respect and spend so much breath inflating other people as he does."

In his Annual Conference Reports as a district superintendent and presiding elder, Brother Van chose not to make just a summary report, but every year he went through the list of each parish in his district, telling what had been accomplished there by the people and the minister the past year. This drew down a certain amount of critical comment, but not from the pastors whose names were spoken aloud on the conference floor with appreciation. Brother Van always found something positive he could say about each pastor and parish in his care. He was careful to see that every one of his ministers got a few kind words said about him at conference, even if he had to "reach" a little bit to do it. If any minister ever needed a dressing down, Brother Van was capable of doing that, but it would be done in private. In public, his utterances were always positive and appreciative.

This practice troubled E. R. Russell some, as he said in a letter, "...the stereotyped expressions that make up the report are the same from year to year, and get on my nerves: 'Brother Haynes has been abundant in labors' etc." Brother Van was not a learned man, and may not have known a hundred different ways to express support and approval. But he was smart enough to know that people respond positively to praise and support. They work harder and feel better when they know their efforts are appreciated, and they like people who enable them to feel good about themselves. Brother Van was "onto" self-esteem long before it became a popular topic.

Self-esteem was what he gave to the people whom he met in the saloons—bartenders, saloon-keepers and their patrons. He didn't give any indication that he ever felt himself superior to any of them, and he accepted them as unique and valuable individuals. People tended to like themselves better when Brother Van was around, and they liked him because of that.

Montana has had many citizens more brilliant than Brother Van, and she has had many men and women of great faith and dedication, but she has never had another who could so effectively and widely influence people for good—all kinds of people in all kinds of places. He lived his powerful faith all day every day; it made his life radiant, and it could not be hidden from others. One friend said, "Whenever Brother Van entered my office, it was as though the shades had been suddenly drawn back, to let the sunshine in."

There was something special about this man. It may have been something in the warmth of his handclasp, the cheerfulness of his greeting, the sincerity of his demeanor, or the heartiness of his personality that made people feel better, and made them determined to make something better of their life. It was probably different things to different people. He was a man of many dimensions, and one person may have responded to different aspects of him than another one would. Whatever it may have been, it was the magic that made him Brother Van, a legendary man, more incredible in reality than in the myths that have grown up around him.

Chapter Nine

...

*A*n abbreviated chronology of
Brother Van's ministry in Montana reveals that for twenty-
nine years without interruption, he served as presiding elder
or district superintendent. District superintendents now, by
comparison, serve a six-year term of office. How he
managed to maintain such a demanding schedule for so
many years without physically caving in is beyond
understanding. From 1872 to 1919 his assignments were:

> 1872-1890 Pastor and Missionary-at-Large
> 1890-1892 Presiding Elder, Great Falls District
> 1892-1897 Superintendent, North Montana Mission
> 1897-1899 Presiding Elder, Helena District
> 1899-1907 Superintendent, North Montana Mission
> 1907-1913 Superintendent, Great Falls District
> 1913-1919 Superintendent, Milk River District

In the 18-year period from 1872 to 1890 he had vast,
first-hand experience as a pastor and missionary, from
which he gained an understanding of the local church and
the life of the parish minister that made him effective as an
administrator. He could not have been as effective in the
years after 1890 if it had not been for the years before,

when he rode a circuit with Riggin, held revivals with Iliff, and plodded long, lonely trails by himself.

The two qualities that suited him so admirably to the years of administrative work were his boundless optimism and his deep sense of brotherliness. He sincerely loved and cared about the ministers and their wives and families, as well as the people in the local churches. People eagerly awaited the time that Brother Van would come to hold Quarterly Conference (an official church business meeting), knowing it would include preaching, singing and good fellowship at a church dinner. He never failed to bring them renewed courage in the task of maintaining the church.

There just were no blues around Brother Van. He knew that God was in the work with them, and it was His will that there be a church in every community. How could they be gloomy? God would prevail. If a minister felt discouraged by the lack of response to his ministerial efforts, Brother Van would come and cheer him up. If he talked of quitting, he reminded him, "Anybody can quit, son. It takes a real man to stay."

He believed that a district superintendent needed to be a wise and fatherly senior pastor who was able to bring hope and help to the pastors, their families and their flock. He knew, from experience, how difficult and lonely a task it could be, being the pastor of a church, and how hard life was on a daily basis for those living on the frontier.

When he came to town, he was expected to preach, and he loved to do it. It gave him the chance to feel personally involved with the churches. It causes the average person to droop with fatigue just to read his journal, in which he kept a careful account of where he preached and the text he preached from in each place. Frequently he also included the number of people present and the amount of the offering that was given. In a journal for 1892-93 that covers about an 18

Brother Van, Presiding Elder,
Age 45.

month period, there are 601 sermons listed—well over one a day! Since he traveled in a wide area, this does not mean 601 different sermons, for he could often use the same sermon in many different communities. Still, the enormous variety of Bible texts listed could not possibly all have lent themselves to the same sermonic content. Just about the only time he could have had to prepare sermons was while he rode the train or stagecoach.

A great deal can be learned about anyone if he or she kept a daily journal that we can examine. Here are a few random entries from Brother Van's journal for 1892-93:

November 23, 1892. Went to Belt. Helpt on the foundation
and arranged for the building of the new church.

Nov. 25. Sabbath morn text Matthew 6:10 41 to sabbath
school evening Mark 8 and 33 Blessed day

Nov. 27 10 o'clock cornerstone laying. God was with us.
Quite a large number were present in this service. Afternoon came to the Falls.

Nov. 29 Choteau Came here this forenoon. Thankgiven.
Bro. Logan preached. I arrived near the close. We had
the grand march the people coming forward and laying
their offering on the altar. Prais God it was good. Took
dinner with Bro. Logans.

Dec. 5th Went to Belt. Bro. Ira Hickory in charge of the
carpenter work. Helpt get men and drove nails in boards
and pushed the work. The church is going up nicely.

Jan. 1, 1893 Took the train at one o'clock and came to
Chinook. Q. Conference. Evening text 2 Peter 1 and
9-10. Communion. I am fully resolved to live nearer to
Jesus this year. Such sweet peace fills my soul.

March 29th Went to Neihart. No pastor for this important
charge.

March 31st Love feast. Text 2 Peter 1 Ch. 9 and 10. Had
great liberty. Afternoon sabbath school. Good evening,
text Luke 13 ch. 18 v. Communion, precious meeting. O
Lord, rais up the right man for this charge

April 2nd Stayd at Monarch until 12 o'clock at night
because of a rail road accident. Mr. Graham was with
me O God save this dear soul.

The spiritual quality that was in his every fiber shines
through in his journals, in such phrases as "precious meeting"
or "Prais God it was good." How deeply he cared for the
pastors, churches and people in general, and how committed

he was to living a Christian life is evident on every page. After more than 20 years on the frontier, his faith was as vibrant as it had been at the start, and it never flagged in all his 47 years of ministry.

At the train stations in his district, it was a common sight to see Brother Van and the local pastor awaiting the arrival of a train late at night. He would spend the evening at one local church, take a late train, and be at his next appointment by morning. Despite having had only a little sleep, he arrived cheerful and bright-eyed, ready for another busy day of visiting, holding meetings and conducting services.

As an administrator, he had many letters to answer, and business to conduct concerning ministerial appointments and church properties. Because his handwriting was poor and his spelling worse, Brother Van had many people around the state who would "write for him," as he called it. E. R. Russell of Fort Benton was one of those secretaries; Leafy Reigel was another. Mr. Russell said, "It takes several persons to meet his demand for secretaries, and when Brother Van visits town, I am Secretary-General, extra-ordinary, irrevocable and no-getting-out-of-it."

Mr. Russell continued: "There is nothing going on in the state now, or that has gone on for the last 37 years, that he does not know about. It is a common thing for several of his preachers to be out of commission with sickness during the year, but you never hear of Brother Van being unable to fill a pulpit engagement. In all the time he has been rustling support for the hospital (in Great Falls) he has never been there himself for treatment. He just keeps going, like a steam engine."

Brother Van was certainly not a model of efficiency in getting his necessary office work done. He would sometimes pause for as long as an hour in the middle of dictating a letter to tell of something amazing or amusing that had taken place during his recent travels.

The life of the traveling preacher was revolutionized by the coming of the railroad. No longer did he have to rely upon a slow-moving horse to get to his appointments. His life was revolutionized again by the advent of the automobile, but Brother Van was distrustful of automobiles from the first and never attempted to learn to drive one. While the automobile made it possible to cover his large territory much more rapidly and thus more frequently, it was a constant source of agony to him. He appreciated the fact that he was no longer bound by train schedules and could go at whatever time he was ready, but he couldn't be convinced that motor cars could really work. Travel by auto was considerably faster and more comfortable than the older forms of transportation, but a lot less reliable. A horse could find his way home through a blinding snowstorm, if you just gave him the reins and let him follow his instincts. By contrast, autos had the annoying habit of breaking down, having flat tires, and running out of gas, leaving the occupants stranded in the most unlikely places at the most inopportune times.

Throughout his career, Will had always been punctuality personified, and he could hardly bear it if he was stranded on the prairie at the time he was expected to be somewhere for a service or a meeting. While the driver tinkered with the car, Brother Van would offer to help, although he knew nothing whatever about the infernal machines, except that they'd rather stop than start. About twice every minute he would pull his watch from his vest pocket, to see if any hope remained for getting to the destination on time.

Gasoline he quaintly referred to as "medicine," for reasons known only to him. As a result of having been stranded more than once simply for lack of fuel, he constantly asked the driver, "Do you have enough medicine?" And at several other points during the journey he could be depended upon to ask it again: "Are you *sure* you've got enough medicine?"

On one occasion a Scobey layman and the local pastor's daughter were driving Brother Van to his next appointment and the girl asked the driver to go fast, wanting to see if Brother Van would be frightened. When he noticed the car gaining speed, he calmly said, "Go ahead and drive as fast as you like. Records show it's the driver who gets hurt worst in car accidents. As for me, I'm prepared to die at any time, and not afraid of it in the least."

His basic distrust of it notwithstanding, the automobile did supplant the train as his basic mode of transportation. The minister or a layman from the town in which he was holding services would usually drive him to the next point on his itinerary. The one thing he did appreciate about the automobile was that it gave him some precious extra time for fellowship with the pastor as they drove across the plains. As automobiles became more reliable, his level of frustration with them was reduced somewhat, but he never did become entirely comfortable with them.

One of the grandest moments in Brother Van's ministry came on August 16, 1912, at the Annual Conference Session in Fort Benton, marking the 40th year of organized Methodism in Montana. It was decided that a special banquet would be held, honoring those Montana pioneer preachers who had served 20 years or more. Besides Brother Van (40 years), that included Francis Riggin (39 years), Job Little (47 years), George Logan (23 years), Jacob Mills (30 years), R. M. Craven (24 years) and J. A. Martin (20 years).

The banquet was at first proposed as an event to honor Brother Van on the occasion of his 40 years in the Montana ministry, but he didn't feel it was right to honor him only, when a couple of others had been there as long or longer, and some others had come very soon after he did. So, with characteristic graciousness, he suggested that all of the pioneers should be honored.

At the banquet, Brother Van and the other senior clergymen told stirring, humorous and exciting stories of some of their most memorable adventures, to the great delight of the large gathering. It was inspiring to the younger preachers to hear those heroic men, and to be reminded of the rich rewards that come with the passing years. They saw clearly that the pioneer ministers, in living what may easily have been called sacrificial lives, had found joys and compensations that far outweighed any sacrifices they had made. Jesus never spoke more truly than when he said, "He that loses his life for my sake shall find it."

Naphtali Luccock, the presiding bishop, was enthusiastic in support of the historical banquet, and suggested the group of pioneers should be called "the Order of Caleb," after those spiritual giants in the Bible who with faith and courage went in and possessed the land of Canaan in the Lord's name. As a special memento of the occasion, each of the pioneer ministers was presented a watch fob charm having a jeweled cross on one side, and the legend "Order of Caleb, Numbers 13:30" engraved on the other side.

A minister who has served 20 years in the Yellowstone (or Montana) conference is eligible for membership, and induction into the Order of Caleb is one of the proudest moments in a minister's life. To be a Caleb is to know that you stand shoulder to shoulder with the giants in Montana's Methodist (and United Methodist) history, the first and greatest of whom was Brother Van.

Of the many honors that came his way, Brother Van was probably most proud of being a member of the Order of Caleb, for it symbolized and summarized his life. He had, indeed, gone in and possessed the land for the Lord, and he had done it in Montana in the companionship of other great and dedicated men. He loved his ministry for the Lord, he loved Montana, and he loved all those men with whom he had worked so long.

In the Methodist Church (now the United Methodist Church), the General Conference, meeting once every four years, is the world-wide legislative body of the church. It is here the Methodist Discipline is written, amended, and revised, and here the denomination's policies and programs are formulated. It is a most important assembly, and Brother Van was a Montana delegate to every General Conference from 1876 until 1916, the last one before his death. In addition, he was made a member of several important committees. Thus, his influence reached beyond the borders of Montana. He became so well known that his picture was featured on the front cover of an issue of *The New York Christian Advocate*, a Methodist monthly magazine.

At some of the later General Conferences, "the heavenly twins," Brother Van and Thomas Iliff, inspired the large assembly with Brother Iliff preaching and Brother Van singing. They were, of course, a big hit with the crowd.

Brother Van went as the Montana delegate to the Methodist centenary celebration at Columbus, Ohio, in July of 1919. Brother Van delighted the large audience with tales of the Methodist preachers in western frontier days. On the evening of July Fourth, a huge "victory parade" was held, and Brother Van was given the special honor of leading the line of march in that procession. Dressed in his western preacher's garb, and mounted on a fine horse, he was in his element. Behind him in the procession were over 10,000 people who spoke, in all, over 100 different languages.

In October of 1893, Brother Van and Francis Riggin had to attend some general church committee meetings in Minneapolis, and one Sunday Riggin preached and Will sang at the Wesley Methodist Church in Minneapolis. They went on from there to spend a number of days at the Chicago

World's Fair. Most of his time in Chicago he spent in going to various churches and preaching services. He did attend the fair some, as he wrote in his journal on October 19: "After dinner went to the fair. Went round of the ferris wheel first thing, 240 feet high, then took the sights in generally. Wonderful things to see and hear at the World's Fair." On a couple of occasions he got to hear Dwight L. Moody preach, and a couple of other times he was not able to get in, as the meeting place was already filled to capacity by the time he arrived.

Brother Van was an avid clipper of items from newspapers and magazines, but he never got around to putting them in order in scrapbooks or elsewhere. He slipped them into his journals and stuffed them into his coat pockets, presumably with the intention of getting them organized someday. In his journals and other personal effects, one finds clippings relating to church dedications and other special church observances as well as articles and clippings relating to commerce, agriculture and railroads, and people involved in such ventures. If someone was elected president of an organization of more than local importance, he received a congratulatory note from Brother Van. Although he was totally dedicated to the church, he was almost as totally dedicated to Montana, and anything affecting his adopted homeland's future and welfare was of real concern to him.

He had the wider kind of vision that makes the church a powerful force in society. Brother Van knew that if the message of the church was to transform society, there had to be Christian people in leadership positions in social, educational, civic, commercial and agricultural groups. He knew they wouldn't all be Methodists, but he hoped they would all be Christian, so he was continually promoting the faith outside of as well as within the church.

Chapter Ten

...

*I*n a lifetime of "boarding 'round," Brother Van was the guest in hundreds of homes, and was certainly one of the most welcome guests who ever came to call in those homes. Whether his visits came unannounced or pre-planned, they were always happy occasions. This was no less true in the parsonage homes than in the homes of the parishioners in which he stayed. He felt most comfortable in homes where the husband and wife had a warm and happy relationship, and he preferred being in homes where there were children. In such cozy surroundings, he felt the joys and comforts that would never be his in a home of his own.

He was not the least impressed with fine china, sterling silver or costly furniture. He had a grand disregard for many of the things women often considered essential in a home, and scarcely took notice of those added touches that comprise the art of homemaking. But he was deeply impressed by the joy of children, and the sense of peace that can be felt so strongly in a happy home.

While there were many of the larger, finer homes in Montana that had a "Brother Van's Room," most families had barely enough room for themselves, and Brother Van was only too happy to be squeezed in by whatever means the family could devise. Frank Hughes of Scobey was a little boy when Brother Van stayed at their home, and he said, "Since our 16 by 16 shack with adobe addition was crowded with a family of seven plus other transient boarders, it was necessary that I sleep with Brother Van. I well remember him kneeling at the bedside for prayer. His balding head caused him more embarrassment than was evident to the outside world. He always carried horehound candy in his vest pocket which he would dampen to touch up his hair. The candy, when wetted, became sticky, and he would swirl his hair around in an attempt to make it cover as much as possible of the bald pate, using the candy to stick it into place."

Late in August of 1910, Brother Van had an appointment to preach at Denton, a little wheat-farming community about 90 miles east of Great Falls. Stepping off the train at Stanford, he still had about 25 miles to travel to the northeast. Since it was the harvest season, he walked over to the grain elevator where farmers brought their grain for temporary storage until the train could transport it to market. He knew that before long, someone from Denton would be there with a load of grain, and he could catch a ride back in the empty wagon. As it turned out, he didn't have to wait at all, because his friend from Denton, Bob Holgate, was unloading his wagon at the time Brother Van walked up. Before the minister could ask for a ride, Bob had already offered him a ride to Denton in his wagon, and invited him to be a guest in their home, three miles south of the town.

Square Butte maintained its ages-long vigil over the rolling hills, all golden with ripening grasses and grains as the wagon creaked and bumped along the trail, and the two occupants conversed amiably. It was well past noon when the wagon finally arrived at the ranch. Will jumped off at the house, while Bob took the team to the barn to unharness and feed them.

Bob's wife, Nelle, came to the door to greet her guest, always a welcome friend at their house. "God bless you, sister," Will's voice boomed out, "What have you got to eat? Bob and I are about done in from hunger!"

"The harvest hands ate just about everything in sight awhile ago," she responded, "but there is lots of fresh gooseberry jam and home-baked bread to hold you until supper time comes around."

"God bless you, sister, bread and gooseberry jam is just what I wanted to eat." So saying, he took a seat at the kitchen table. In a minute or two, Bob came into the house, and the two men ate an alarming quantity of the bread and jam. Nelle prepared a large quantity of tasty food for the evening meal, and when everyone finished eating and the dishes were done, Bob and Nelle and their son Stanley climbed into the wagon with Brother Van for the short ride to the church in Denton.

Nelle commented, "That dark cloud off to the southwest looks like it could mean business. We may be glad I brought these blankets along."

"Send the rain, Lord, send the rain," Brother Van hooted gleefully. His thirty-eight years in Montana had taught him two things about the weather. First, he learned that rain was always welcome and needed at any time of the year in that dry-land country. Second, he had learned that one cannot fight the weather. One's schedule must go on, rain or shine. If it rains, you just make the best you can of a rainy day, and rejoice in the moisture.

The Lord had ears for the plea, for rain soon came, in torrents. Still about a mile from town, the four sought refuge momentarily under the blankets Nelle had brought, but they were soon so drenched they afforded little protection. When all four were huddled in the wagon, dripping wet, Brother Van began to sing "There shall be showers of blessing, send them upon us, O Lord."

Usually a rain such as this passes through an area in an hour or less, but on this night the storm cloud hovered over the community and the surrounding area without moving on toward the east. The little meeting house in Denton contained only a half-dozen people that night; most of those who might have come had foreseen what the weather conditions would be and had wisely opted not to venture out. But to Brother Van, a congregation of even one presented an evangelistic opportunity, and he wasn't disturbed by the small turnout. They built a fire in the heating stove so they could get themselves dried off a little, and at eight o'clock, as scheduled, the service began. Brother Van distributed his travel-worn song books and everyone enjoyed singing some favorite hymns. By popular request, Brother Van sang some of his special hymns and gospel songs, and then he delivered the sermon he had planned for the evening. People forgot it was raining outdoors, as they became engrossed in the way Brother Van challenged them to live nearer to Christ, and to commit themselves more fully to showing his love and forgiveness toward others. When the service was over and they looked outdoors, they could see the rain hadn't abated much. Nobody felt like heading for home and getting soaked and chilled again. It hadn't been much fun the first time, and by now it would be even more chilly. After a brief intermission, the minister called the people back to order, and there followed a marathon, free-wheeling session of preaching, praying, singing and laughing together that lasted until three in the morning, with only a few brief pauses to look outside and see if it was still raining.

Day was breaking as the wagon pulled into the Holgate yard, and everyone was hungry. "What would you like to eat, Brother Van?" Nelle inquired, "It's nearly breakfast time, and we may as well eat something before we go to bed."

"You folks have whatever you like. I think I'll just have some eggs and milk."

"How would you like them fixed?" his hostess inquired.

"Fixed? No need to fix them at all." Taking a bowl of farm-fresh eggs, he broke six of them directly into his mouth, swallowing each one in a gulp, some of the white dribbling off his chin. Then, wiping his mouth, he drank a quart of milk and headed for bed. In his long life as a bachelor, he had acquired a few eating habits that were shocking or even repulsive to others, and this was certainly one of them.

Not all of his experiences on the long trail were as pleasant as the one with the Holgate family. Once he stayed in a home where he was given a place to sleep in the attic. It was summer, and the space was just barely large enough for a man to lie down, with practically nothing left over. Brother Van felt sure he wouldn't survive that night, but he didn't know if he would be dead of suffocation or of claustrophobia. Lacking a spare room, many homes could afford nothing more than floor space in the living room for extra guests. Brother Van spent many a night on the floor, with a buffalo robe under and over him.

Caught in a winter storm one day, he was forced to take refuge at the first place he came to, which turned out to be a hovel. Most frontier families knew that being poor was never an excuse for being dirty, but this one did not. The structure was so crude that it was only a little bit warmer inside than it was outside, and Will slept that night under a buffalo robe with all his clothing on. The next morning he used his standard tactic for evading food that might be of questionable character by saying to his hostess, "Sister, I'm not hard to please. I like my potatoes boiled with the skins on, and my eggs cooked in the shell."

Brother Van really appreciated good food, and he gravitated toward the warmth of the kitchen from which emanated the

*Brother Van, right, greets Rev. W.A. Shannon. The Presiding
Elder greeted many who responded to the call to serve
beside him on the Montana frontier.*

delightful odors of food cooking. At dinner, he always had
trouble making the biscuits and honey come out even, and
he was particularly fond of "roastin' ears," as he called corn
on the cob. While he used to get joshed about the pile of
cobs beside his plate, it never embarrassed him enough to
deter him from eating just one more. He was also fond of
fried chicken, as every good Methodist minister was supposed
to be. But, in all his years of travel, he was served "company
fare" so often that he finally got his fill of chicken. In his

later years, he preferred roast beef if it was available, but he still usually got chicken.

Besides liking to swallow eggs whole and raw, another of his bad eating habits was that he "slurped" his soup. This often caused youngsters a lot of grief in homes he visited. Then as now, children were taught by their mothers that you must not slurp your soup, but here was everyone's idol, Brother Van, doing it. He ate his soup with the same zest he did everything else, and slurping was quite unavoidable in that case. But many a youngster was sent away from the table for creating a scene while Brother Van ate his soup. One wise hostess simply decided that whenever he was a guest, she would serve no soup with dinner. Brother Van seemed not to be trainable with regard to eating his soup, but the problem could be sidestepped simply enough.

Children in a home always knew that a visit by Brother Van would be an event to remember. They were drawn to him as if he were the Pied Piper. It was not a one-sided thing, for he loved the children, too. Gathering as many as he could into his arms and on his lap, he would begin to sing, clapping his hands in rhythm:

> Happy on the way.
> Happy on the way;
> Praise the Lord,
> I'm happy on the way.

Of course, the children would join in the singing and the clapping with great enthusiasm. He had to snicker up his coat sleeve one day when he heard a youngster paraphrase the song, singing, "Praise Brother Van, I'm happy on the way."

The E. R. Russell children of Fort Benton were playing in the back yard one day when Brother Van arrived, hoping to get their father to do some secretarial work for him. The children demanded that he must taste the mud pies they had just made, frosted with red brick dust and prettily fringed with dandelion leaves, and Brother Van bravely obliged them.

He taught the children many songs. He had some motions to accompany the popular song, "The Gospel Train is Coming." They also loved to sing "You Must Not Work on Sunday." Especially he taught them his simple "rules of life," a kind of simplified set of commandments:

> Mind your ma and pa.
> Know where your hat and books are.
> Pray.
> Read the Bible.
> Go to Sunday school.
> Never tell a lie.

The children took him seriously, and remembering these things had a great influence on many lives. Brother Van, knowing the children would remember the commandment about one's hat and books, would often say, as he was getting ready to leave, "Now, I wonder where my hat is?" Of course he knew where it was, but so did the children, and when one of them would triumphantly bring it to him, he would make a great show of being pleased and surprised to have it found so quickly. And he would laugh with great appreciation if they reminded him that you're supposed to always know where your hat is.

When he was a visitor in a home, before bed there would be family devotions, even if the family didn't have them on a regular basis. He would ask if they could read a few verses from the Bible and have a prayer before going to bed, and the host family, of course, would be only too glad to do that. He rarely led these himself, but a family member would read a few verses from the Bible, and another would offer a prayer.

At its close, Brother Van would say, "Amen! That was a good prayer." He made everyone feel at ease and comfortable about doing this, even if it was a new custom to them. Some families no doubt were influenced in this way to close each day with the reading of a few verses of scripture and a prayer.

His visits in people's homes sometimes led to new commitments to the Christian life. More than once, his way of living, so happy and full of peace, succeeded in helping people turn to Christ when his preaching had not. In Miles City, he often stayed at the Haynes home. They were a Presbyterian family, but two of the Haynes boys grew up to become Methodist ministers and worked alongside Brother Van for many years. The testimony of Brother Van's daily life had been the most persuasive force leading to their commitment to enter the ministry.

You could generally hear Brother Van coming before you could see him, for it was his custom to be singing some joyous Christian song as he walked or rode along. A little boy was said to have come home and announced, "Mother, there's going to be church tonight. I was over at Tommy's and we heard Brother Van go by, singing." His singing often replaced a knock on the door to announce his arrival.

Mrs. Allan Rodger, the widow of one of the early pioneer Methodist ministers, told of the unusual way in which she first met Brother Van. A stranger approached the parsonage door, singing as he came. The Reverend Allen Rodger was out on parish work and she was home alone, but she let the stranger in because it was raining. Inside, Will made known his identity, and she did her best to make him feel welcome and at home. As it continued to rain, the roof began to leak. First there was just a random drop here and there; then the leaks became more numerous and greater in volume. Finally, water was coming down indoors almost as strongly as it was

outdoors. Sister Rodger got her umbrella and the two of them
sat under it in the driest part of the house, while Brother Van
sang:

> Then cheer, my sister, cheer,
> The time will soon be o'er;
> Our loved ones we shall meet, we'll greet
> Upon the Golden Shore.

Whether it was a disdain for things relating to the physical
aspects of life, or sheer, total ignorance about what most
people felt to be important in a home, the fact is that Brother
Van apparently lacked the capacity to evaluate the parsonages
within his district, and this was perhaps his most serious short-
coming as a church administrator. It caused a lot of trouble for
a good many preachers, and especially for their wives. Paul M.
Adams was a fledgling minister when he and his wife were
being assigned to Utica. Paul asked Brother Van about the
parsonage, and was told, "Oh, Utica has a good parsonage—
well-furnished, too."

Adams said, "We traveled from Virginia City halfway across
Montana to find a frame shack built by an amateur carpenter
out of green lumber, which, in shrinking, had left numerous
cracks half an inch wide. These had furnished refuge for abundant bedbugs until we had reduced their number in nightly
battles. For furnishing there was not much. A crudely
constructed table about ten feet long was in the kitchen. There
was a cook stove and a heating stove, and there were two
beds, which we shared with the bugs. There were no floor
coverings at all.

"On his first visit, Brother Van preached at Utica and then I
drove him to Garneill, 20 miles away. I was to be gone all
night, and had left my wife at home sick, but he seemed to
take all that in stride. On the way over, he said, 'Do you think

I misrepresented the parsonage situation to you? Sometimes I am told I am not exactly truthful about these things.'

" 'No,' I replied, 'but you were too optimistic.' The truth of the matter was that, being a bachelor, a roof over his head was sufficient and all else was glorious. He had no conception at all of what a woman would consider to be essential in a home." Unfortunately, or perhaps fortunately, we have no inkling of what manner of bachelor dwelling Brother Van maintained for himself, or in company with Francis Riggin or others. Knowing his disregard for such mundane things, plus some of his unsavory eating habits, one can imagine that his quarters may have been a frightful sight to behold. On the other hand, knowing how important it was to him to always make a neat and clean appearance, it is just as easy to imagine that he kept his quarters very presentable at all times.

Brother Van had two tricks that he used for "remembering" names. His memory was actually quite phenomenal, but he met so many people in so many places, it was not possible to remember each one always. Seeing a familiar face with which he could not put a name, he would ask the person walking with him, "Quick! What's this fellow's name?" Getting the name from his companion, Brother Van would greet him by name, and the friend would often reply with words such as, "Good morning, Brother Van. What a great memory you have! We haven't met in 12 years, and yet you remembered my name."

"Yes, brother," Will would reply, "there are many mysteries in Providence."

The second ploy he made use of at times was to simply ask the person his name. If he said his name was Johnson, Brother Van would say, "Oh, I remembered it was Johnson, but I couldn't think of your first name." If the person gave his first name, he would say, "I remembered your name was Ed, but I can't think of your last name."

One of the remarkable things about Brother Van is that he was never seen to give way to a display of bad temper, no matter how greatly provoked. His faith that God was guiding the destiny of all human affairs enabled him to view the cares and tribulations of earth as being of little real consequence. He lived zestfully, and the constant sparkle of good humor in his eyes was in testimony to the faith that was deep in his heart. Brother Van enjoyed a good laugh, even at his own expense. Often, he was the prankster.

Riding with a tenderfoot preacher in a box wagon, Brother Van was approaching the central Montana mining town of Gilt Edge. When they topped a rise and started down a long, steep slope, they saw another wagon ahead of them, proceeding very slowly with a heavy load of logs. The driver had locked the rear wheels, causing them to drag rather than turn, which acted as brakes for the vehicle. Wise to the ways of the West, Brother Van recognized at once what the situation was. You didn't dare to let a heavy load pick up speed on a downhill slope, or there would be a disastrous wreck. The trail was too narrow for another wagon to pass, so Brother Van settled his team into a slow pace behind the logging wagon. The neophyte preacher, new to the West, exclaimed, "Look, Brother Van! The rear wheels of that wagon aren't turning. Do you suppose the driver knows it?"

Repressing his mirth, the veteran preacher replied, "I guess he must not. Wheels are round so they'll roll, aren't they? Maybe you'd better jump down and run ahead and tell him." The unsuspecting youth did so, eager to do his good turn for the day. He returned in a moment, having learned that the driver indeed knew the wheels weren't turning, and it was purely intentional that they weren't. Brother Van laughed uproariously, and soon his young companion joined in, wiser to the ways of the West and the wiles of Brother Van.

Bill Cook of Choteau was the driver of the stagecoach on

the route from Choteau to the Canadian border, and Will rode
that stage on many occasions. When the seat up high beside
the driver was vacant, he preferred to sit there, instead
of being inside the coach where you couldn't see very much
of the scenery. After riding and chatting awhile, the preacher
would say, "Let's sing, Bill."

Mr. Cook said, "Then Brother Van would start to sing,
letting his grand voice roll out across the prairie in some
favorite hymn. You would sure want to sing then, even if you
couldn't. I vow that sometimes you could have heard him
three miles away!"

Although he was born in Pennsylvania, Brother Van was a
Montanan at heart from the first moment he arrived. His
loyalty and devotion to Montana was second only to his
dedication to the Lord. While he and Paul Adams, the pastor
at Utica, were driving in a horse and wagon to Garneill, they
stopped at a ranch house to visit a man Will knew. In the
course of the conversation, the man revealed his plans to
spend the coming winter back East. Will expressed his disap-
proval of such a notion. Standing up in the wagon, he raised
his arm, spiraling his index finger to the sky, and said, "To
me, Montana is next to heaven, and I'm never going to leave
Montana until I go straight up! Drive on, Brother Adams."
There was no point in continuing to talk to someone with so
little loyalty to Montana!

He was never an admirer from afar. He worked for the
state's welfare in a good many ways throughout his long
career. For years he served on the State Board of Charities by
the appointment of several governors. He was the friend and
confidant of every territorial and state governor of Montana
from the time of his arrival until his death. Upon arriving in
the capital city, he would go directly to the governor's office.
He was always welcomed warmly and was usually invited to
have lunch with the governor. He was always an advocate for

what was best for Montana, whether or not it directly
involved the church or religion.

Because of his friendship with the governor, as well as his
untiring work on committees involving the state, Brother Van
was the natural choice to deliver the prayer of invocation at
the ceremony dedicating the new state capitol. Brother Van
was, after all, more widely known and more generally loved
than the governor himself. It didn't do a governor's reputation
any harm to be known as a friend of Brother Van's! Montana
had been admitted to statehood in November, 1889, and that
had been a proud moment for Brother Van. Being involved in
the dedication of the capitol was another high point, because,
as he said, to him, Montana was next to heaven.

His circle of friends included the clergy and their families,
the members of their flocks, governors, judges, legislators of
the state, patrons and proprietors of saloons, farmers and
stockmen, cowboys and Indians. In short, it included
everyone. It was entirely fitting that he was called by many
"the best-loved man in Montana."

Chapter Eleven

...

Not content just to build churches and parsonages and organize new congregations in more than a hundred Montana communities, Brother Van had concerns as wide and varied as the needs of mankind. Whenever he became aware of a need that he believed the Methodists had the capacity to do something about, he did his best to push them to the task with the battle cry, "Under God, brethren, this must be done!"

The total strength of Methodism in Montana was six ministers and less than 150 church members in 1877 when a resolution was passed calling for the establishment of a university, and Brother Van was a member of the committee that would work to give life to the resolution. For eleven years the committee made plans and studied every aspect of the situation, receiving and rejecting several offers of land for possible building sites. In 1888 they accepted the offer of a group of Helena laymen, who would donate a 205 acre tract in the valley north of Helena if the Methodist conference would raise $50,000 for an initial building to start the college.

When district superintendent R. E. Smith was named president of the college that existed only in the hearts of the Montana pastors, they personally subscribed the $2000 to pay his first year's salary. Brothers Van and Riggin, co-pastors of the Fort Benton circuit, pledged $100 each, while the salary paid them in the past year had been just $300 each. The subscription list for the president's salary contained 31 names, of whom 27 were ministers and their wives.

Following the lead of Brother Van, Montana Methodist pastors have always had the attitude that the development of the church in the state is the task of the committed clergy. They would not wait until there were enough laymen ready and willing to do the job; by that time the moment of greatest opportunity might be past. Montana today is a better place by far because Montana Methodism made some daring ventures of faith in the early years, entering into projects that could not possibly support themselves, and establishing new work when there was no one in sight to lead it. They didn't often ask, "Can we do it?" They only asked, "Does it need to be done? Is it important and worth giving a sacrificial effort?" Brother Van often persuaded them that if God wanted a thing done, He would open the way for its achievement. He would be the potter, if the Montana ministers would just be willing to be the clay.

By the fall of 1890, a five-story building awaited the forty students who enrolled for classes at Montana Wesleyan University. All under one roof were dormitory rooms for men and women, the dining facilities, classrooms and offices. A faculty of high caliber had been secured. Enrollment was expected to hit the magical mark of 100 in 1893, but the economic panic of that year reduced the number to only seven. Somehow the school survived. Students were accepted for high-school level and even grade school level work.

Farms and ranches were often so remote from the towns that getting to school daily was a great hardship or was just not possible for a good many. Such children, if enrolled at Montana Wesleyan, could get a quality education and be living under Christian supervision, making it possible for parents to send their children there with confidence.

Montana Wesleyan University was plagued with problems from the outset. Some influential ministers in the conference did not support the idea of sponsoring a college, and at many points in the early days the trustees would have abandoned the project, had it not been for Brother Van's unyielding persistence. With tears in his eyes, he would stand before them and say, "Under God, brethren, we must not abandon this project!" He would ask them to get on their knees while he led them in prayer, asking the Lord to give them courage equal to the tasks before them, and he would keep on praying until he knew they had come over to his side. It seemed that every time Brother Van turned his back, someone would introduce a motion to close the college, and he would have to come before them again, pleading, weeping, praying and cajoling until the motion was withdrawn.

Thinking they could attract more local students and that going to the college would be more attractive to others if it was right in town instead of out in the country, the college left the valley location and operated in the city of Helena until 1935. Prospects never seemed more fair, with 237 students in 1932. But an earthquake in 1935 so severely damaged the college building that it had to be abandoned. The students had gathered in the gymnasium to celebrate a football victory on the eve of October 18 when the earthquake struck. Most of them took refuge in the middle of the floor, and no one was injured, although many were narrowly missed by falling debris.

In 1936, the college merged with Billings Polytechnic Institute, and the newly-formed school was named Rocky Mountain College. It is still the only Protestant church-related college within a 600 mile radius of Billings. It flourishes still, with around 500 full-time students, numerous fine modern

*A mountain congregation typical of those to whom
Brother Van preached and sang
throughout Montana.*

buildings, and a highly competent, professional faculty. Brother
Van could not have foreseen the tortuous trail his college
would travel, but he was right, beyond doubt, when he said,
"Under God, brethren, the school must not be closed."

Brother Van knew the importance of a hospital as a public
institution, where competent medical care often spells the
difference between life and death. Throughout his career, he
had seen too much of death and knew that many deaths
could have been prevented, if proper care had been available.
Jennie had suffered and died, and his sister, too, at far too
early an age. There were some compelling reasons why
Brother Van was one of the principal figures in the
establishment of the deaconess hospital work in Montana.
He may or may not have been the first person to envision

the church sponsoring a hospital, but there is no doubt whatever that he was the most steadfast supporter and most tireless salesman for the cause.

In all, seven hospitals came into being, resulting from the conference resolution to establish a hospital that was made in 1896. Beginning with a $6,000 donation from James J. Hill, president of the Great Northern Railway Company, a hospital building with 20 beds was constructed in Great Falls. In Brother Van's lifetime, other deaconess hospitals were established in Glasgow, Sidney, Bozeman and Butte. After his death, hospitals in Billings and Havre opened their doors. The Glasgow, Butte and Sidney hospitals have since become community hospitals, but those located in Great Falls, Billings, Bozeman and Havre are still known as Deaconess hospitals.

Deaconesses were women, usually nurses or teachers, who had full professional training and credentials. They had dedicated themselves to a Christian vocation of service, and they worked without salary, as a rule, receiving only their board and room and perhaps a small clothing allowance as recompense for their total commitment. While Brother Van and others were avid supporters and promoters, the success of the hospitals could in no way have occurred without the tireless self-sacrifice of the deaconesses.

The deaconesses knew that Brother Van was their best friend and that his was the support that they could rely on. His was the push and the lift that was still there when everyone else had grown weary of pushing and lifting. The four Deaconess hospitals in Montana today, at Havre, Great Falls, Bozeman and Billings, are all major medical centers serving their respective regions of the state. They have the latest equipment and provide the highest quality of professional care. They are no longer staffed by deaconesses, but they do still have a relationship with the United Methodist Church.

But of all the institutions in his life, the one dearest to Brother Van's heart was the children's home in Helena. We do not know if it was his idea originally, but there is no doubt that he was its most ardent supporter. The building out in the valley that had been the original home of the college was abandoned and falling to ruin. Having cost $50,000 to build, it now looked as though $50 would be too much to ask for it. More than once, Brother Van could have been seen kneeling amid the weeds that covered the grounds around the decaying, almost windowless, building, pleading with the Lord to show them the way to make use of this property. It was a black eye for the church. People had called it "Van Orsdel's folly," and he was determined that it would be returned to Christian service.

It was 1909, and the Methodist conference had trouble enough on its hands with trying to keep the college afloat. They had little enthusiasm for adding yet another financial burden such as a children's home would be, but Brother Van had adopted the cause, and he would not give up. Several powerful ministers opposed him, but he insisted, "Under God, brethren, we must have a Montana Deaconess School!" He was not blind to the opposition, nor did he fail to understand their reluctance to take on yet another burden, but he seemed to know what they did not—a children's home would strike a responsive note in the people of the state. People love children, and their heart naturally goes out to unfortunate ones.

From the start, it was easier to raise $100 for the children's home than $10 for the college. Children who were orphans or were innocent victims of other types of family tragedy deserved the opportunity to live in a secure and loving Christian environment and to receive a good education. They were Montana's future, and the enterprise met at once with solid public support.

Presiding Elder W. W. Van Orsdel (age 52) always had his bag packed, ready for travel.

Miss Louise Stork, a deaconess, was secured as superinten-dent, and 5 other deaconesses came to assist her as faculty members and house mothers. Brother Van always came to the Montana Deaconess School when he was in Helena, and the children and deaconesses alike came to look forward to his visits. He loved to come at mealtime, going down the stairs leading to the dining room as he sang "Harvest Time" or another of his favorite songs. Before he came into view, they all knew he had come for a visit, and they began to sing with him, eagerly awaiting the moment his beloved hulk would appear in the doorway. He was like a father to them. He naturally loved all children, but for these who had no families, or who came from dysfunctional homes and broken families, he had a special measure of love.

Brother Van lived to see the Montana Deaconess School through the first decade of its existence. It was firmly founded, well-managed, and has never been a financial burden on the Methodist church, nor any other church in Montana. The children there now go to the regular public schools in Helena, but the home—today called The Intermountain Children's Home—still provides a secure and happy place for children to live who have had some kind of misfortune in their home life, making it necessary for them to reside in another type of setting.

Montana was and is one of the most sparsely populated states, so in order to get many important things done, it needs to make up in faith and daring what it lacks in numerical strength. When the Deaconess School was founded, it was the only institution of its kind between Chicago and the West Coast. The demand for services was so great that the school was immediately filled to capacity and other applicants had to be turned away.

Brother Van knew better than most others that there is no substitute for a sound Christian home. But, when misfortune makes the ideal entirely impossible, the church ought to be there, he believed, offering a helping hand, providing a place where children can be safe and happy and be nurtured in the Christian faith.

Montana owes an incalculable debt to the rock-ribbed tenacity, or call it pure Dutch stubbornness, if you will, of Brother Van. When he became convinced that a thing ought to be done, and in the sight of God he could not be pardoned for turning his back on such a need, he went ahead by faith. He knew that God found ways to get those things done that He wanted done, and people either had to push or pull or get out of the way. Montana would be poorer by dozens of Methodist churches, several hospitals, a college and a children's home had it not been for Brother Van's dauntless faith and Dutch tenacity.

Others were often concerned that Brother Van was pushing them into taking hold of more opportunities than they could possibly make good on. Time has proved they were wrong and Brother Van was right. The college, the hospitals and the children's home have made enormous contributions to the general welfare and life of Montana. If Montana Methodists had not risen to the challenge in early years, who would have? Others might have, but there's no guarantee of it. And others would surely have done it later, perhaps missing out on some good opportunities thereby.

History never remembers the ones who said it couldn't be done, who weren't even willing to try. It remembers fondly and proudly people like Brother Van, who do not run away from problems, but look them full in the face and say, "Under God, we must do something about this!" Brother Van felt that ignorance and death, and the suffering of little children in broken homes could not be allowed to go on unchallenged. These things create human waste, human suffering, and pain, and something ought to be done about it. We can do something to reduce the amount of ignorance in the world, and to protect and preserve life, and to give children a chance to have a happy childhood and a Christian upbringing. To do so we must and we will have a college and some hospitals and a children's home.

While others said, "How could we possibly do such a thing?" Brother Van said, "How could we possibly not do such a thing? Under God, brethren, we must not let this opportunity for service pass us by."

Chapter Twelve

•••

*B*rother Van spent a lifetime setting records and departing from custom. Although he was straight-laced, old-fashioned, and very strict and unyielding about some things, he was, by nature, an innovator, doing things that hadn't been done before, or in ways they hadn't been done before. In his 1905 journal he tells of having a song and prayer service by telephone, with most of a community taking part by simply taking their telephones off the hook, since all were on the same large party line. Brother Van was making use of tele-conferences before anyone had ever heard of such a thing!

He spoke to people where he found them, even in saloons. He sang as much as he preached and sometimes more. Half of the things he did, it seems, had never been done before.

He was always aggressive, but not arrogant. He believed the Lord deserved all the credit for anything that W. W. Van Orsdel had accomplished. In later years, many honors were bestowed upon him, such as an honorary doctorate from the college he helped to found. He clearly preferred being Brother Van over being Dr. Van Orsdel. The recognition and adulation did not make him swell-headed. He was what we would call a "ham," perhaps. He said very little, himself, about his work, but he liked to have others say good things about him and what he had done. He loved everybody and hungered for their love.

Although he enjoyed his popularity, he was secure enough within himself that he could stand honest criticism, if it was given by someone he trusted. George "Dad" Logan, one of Brother Van's long-time fellow ministers, said, "I could never stir him to resentment by finding fault with his manner of saying and doing things, but let someone attempt criticism with an air of superiority, and you would see his bristles rise in a minute. He never spoke an evil word against his preachers, nor would he allow one preacher to criticize another in his presence. He used kind, even flattering words in all his dealings with people whether socially or in regard to his work. . . .I have traveled with him by stagecoach, by rail and by private conveyance alone with him on the prairies, miles from human habitation, but I have never heard him utter a word that could not be spoken in the presence of ladies, in homes of Christian culture and refinement."

Because Brother Van was so widely known and so well-loved, his birthday, in later years, was made into quite a celebration. He arranged his schedule so he could be in Fort Benton on or near the 20th of March for the community-wide observance. Fort Benton was probably as much home to him as anywhere in Montana, for he had first landed in Montana at Fort Benton, and had served that parish with Francis Riggin. Some of his longest friendships were with Fort Benton people.

Light-hearted, fun-filled entertainments were the highlight of the birthday celebrations. Children recited verses and sang songs. Brother Van was always given the opportunity to share some of his pioneer recollections, and he would be bombarded with requests to sing some of his most special songs, such as "Harvest Time" and "Diamond in the Rough."

And each year one or more special songs or poems were written by local people for the occasion. Typical of such offerings was the one written by Mrs. E. R. Russell in honor of Brother Van's birthday in 1915. It was read as a lead-in to the presentation of a cash gift that had been raised by a public collection, under the sponsorship of the Ladies Aid of the Fort Benton Methodist Church:

We are very glad to greet you, Brother Van,
And we've come tonight to tell as best we can
How we all have missed you sore,
And we're glad you've come once more,
As you've done in years before, Brother Van.

When the March winds bluster round us, Brother Van,
Then we all begin to wonder, to a man;
Will he meet us here again
When his birthday comes, and then
Hurry back again, Brother Van?

Then we wonder what we'll give you, Brother Van.
Think of slippers, yes, and handkerchiefs and tan
Hose and black ones, but we fear
That with Christmas passed so near,
You have many, or 'tis queer, Brother Van.

Oh, we wonder what you most want, Brother Van.
An auto, or a Ford, or just a span
Of fine horses that can go,
How we'd really like to know,
So that we our love might show, Brother Van.

We all know your pockets leak, Brother Van.
Not because they're worn and holey, no, but man,

You can't see a friend in need,
And not help him out in deed;
You're always sowing seed, Brother Van.

Will you please accept this small gift, Brother Van?
Give it place in some pet scheme, perhaps, or plan?
May it help some burden bear,
May it lighten some small care, and
In your joy we'll have a share, Brother Van.

May your years be long and useful, Brother Van,
And your harvest rich and fruitful as it can;
God be with you all the way,
May he lead you night and day,
'Till "Well done" the King shall say, Brother Van.

We have loaned you to the whole church, Brother Van,
And we've prayed that God would bless you as you ran;
They have added a D. D.
To your good old name, we see,
But to us you'll always be Brother Van.

One can readily imagine the intense pleasure such things gave Brother Van, and how such a sincere expression of affection must have brought tears to his eyes. Life had not provided him the joys of a home and family life, but Brother Van had a very large family of people of all ages who loved him everywhere he went. In that respect he was, and he considered himself to be, the richest man in Montana.

It is not at all likely that he really cared whether anyone knew his age, but he had a lot of fun trying to keep it a secret. On the occasion of his 69th birthday, the *Great Falls Daily Tribune* reported:

"The _____th? birthday of Rev. W. W. Van Orsdel, superintendent of the Milk River District of the Methodist Church, generally known as 'Brother Van,' was celebrated last evening at Fort Benton. Just how old Brother Van is, is the great mystery of the Methodist Church in Montana."

A year later, in 1918, it seemed the secret was about to be revealed. Some newspapers, hinted, accurately, that he was now eligible to join a "three score and ten" club. One of the minister's old-time friends in Fort Benton, Miss Anna Taylor, age 94, was present at his birthday party, and she asked him, straight out, how old he was. Miss Anna was very hard of hearing, so everyone quieted down, knowing the preacher would have to shout to make her hear his reply. What he shouted to her was, "I'm going to tell you sometime, Anna, but I don't want to tell it in front of all these young people."

At this same 70th birthday party in Fort Benton, the now-famous letter from Charles M. Russell was read. Having been selected for jury duty in Great Falls, Russell couldn't come to the party, so he sent the letter, which was headed with his original sketch of a steamboat standing in abeyance while a great herd of buffalo crossed the Missouri River. In the first part of the letter, Russell recounts his first meeting with Brother Van, and he concludes with these wonderful, lyrical lines,

I have met you many times since then, Brother Van—sometimes in lonely places, but you were never lonesome or alone, for a man with scarred hands and feet stood beside you and near him there is no hate. All you met loved you.

Be good and you'll be happy is an old saying which many contradict and say goodness is a rough trail over dangerous passes with windfalls and swift, deep rivers to cross. I have never ridden it very far myself, but judging from the looks of you, it's a cinch bet that with a hoss called faith under you it's a smooth, flower-grown trail with easy fords, where birds sing and cold, clear streams dance in the sunlight all the way to the pass that crosses the big divide.

Brother Van, you have ridden that trail a long time, and I hope you still ride to many birthdays on this side of the big range.

With best wishes from my best half and me,

Your Friend,

C. M. Russell

Russell's wish was not to be granted. There would be only one more birthday "this side of the big range."

A reception honoring Brother Van and the local pastor and his wife, The Reverend and Mrs. J. A. Hill, was to be held in Chinook the evening of October 8, 1919. Will had spent most of the day at the Reigel home (Leafy and her family had moved to Chinook from their sawmill at Landusky), dictating letters to Miss Leafy and getting caught up on his administrative chores. When he had completed the dictation, it was time for them to go to the church for the evening activities, but he couldn't get his arm to go into his coat sleeve. Leafy asked him what was wrong, and he said, "Nothing's wrong, I just can't get my arm into my coat," and then he fell to the floor, unconscious.

Leafy was able to get a doctor to come at once, and after a short while, Brother Van regained consciousness. Leafy and the doctor moved him to his bedroom upstairs, where the doctor did a thorough examination and said it was his opinion that Brother Van had suffered a stroke. His brain didn't seem to have been affected, but the left side of his face

*Brother Van (age 70) in a pose taken a year
or so before his death.*

and his left arm and leg were severely paralyzed. From the
first, the minister whose life had been a study in perpetual
motion, insisted he felt good enough to get up and be about
his business. He gamely tried to get up, but he could not
force his arm and leg to move.

All those around him were in a state of grief, of course.
The Reverend John Martin came from Great Falls to see Will,
and said of it later: "It was heartbreaking to see our
ministerial lifelong friend lying in a stupor and perfectly

helpless. May God spare him to us for a little more counsel and inspiration, and the songs that have cheered us on in many a dreary day."

News of Brother Van's stroke spread like wildfire throughout the state; every news publication, whether it was published daily or weekly, carried the most recent medical bulletin regarding the famous patient's condition. As might have been expected for one so widely known and greatly loved, cards, letters, telegrams and flowers came to the Reigel home daily in prodigious quantities.

The doctor believed his famous patient was too ill to be moved, so Brother Van remained for more than a week at the Reigel home, where he was receiving the best of professional care. The deaconess in charge of the hospital in Glasgow came to Chinook on the train to personally tend him. Will's brother, Fletcher, was doing evangelistic work in northeast Montana, teamed with Tommy Rogers, Will's long-time friend from Oil City, Pennsylvania. As soon as they heard of Will's illness, Fletcher and Tommy dropped everything and came to his side. Bishop R. J. Cooke adjourned the Annual Conference a day early in North Dakota so he would have time to pay a visit to Brother Van.

Those keeping watch by the bedside did not think it strange to see the bishop in tears as he knelt to lead them in prayer, expressing how they all loved this dear man, and how fervently they asked for his recovery. But it soon became clear that if he did recover, he would remain almost completely helpless. His arm and leg wouldn't work, but his mind still did, and his ministry was still the thing uppermost on Will's mind. John Martin had been hastily appointed to oversee Brother Van's district during his illness, and whenever Martin came into the sick room, the first question to him was "John, how are you off for preachers?" Then, as long as his strength held out, he would question Martin about events in the churches.

Nine days after his stroke, on October 17, the doctor felt his patient was able to travel to Great Falls, where he would be placed in the Deaconess Hospital he had been instrumental in establishing. Although he was faithful about visiting the deaconesses and the patients in the hospital when he came to Great Falls, Brother Van had never before been there as a patient. He remained there 63 days.

At first, under the loving and capable care of Miss Augusta Ariss and the other deaconesses, Brother Van showed some slight improvement. Miss Ariss wrote:

> We all felt the honor and the sacredness of the task of caring for him, whose life so pure and godly had been the inspiration that held us to the service. What greater blessing or privilege could come to a servant in the work than that of caring for this chosen man of God? His room was a veritable gateway to heaven; his smile, his gratitude, his patient suffering, his holy joy, his words of cheer, will never be forgotten by the nurses who tenderly cared for him. . . .

Just after the first of December, his strength began to ebb; day by day he lost ground in the battle for life. By the middle of December even Brother Van knew the end was near. He made some plans for his funeral service and appointed a committee of persons very dear to him to plan the rest and carry it out: the Reverend John Martin, the Reverend Philo Haynes, the Reverend E. L. White, and Miss Leafy Reigel. The serenity and strength with which he faced the entire ordeal of his illness and finally his death was abundant proof that the faith he had preached for more than half a century was very real to him. The funeral service was to be a final testimony to that kind of faith. To die full of faith and hope in the Lord was the highest end of all living, and for him death held no fears whatever. The funeral should be a celebration, he felt, not a sad and mournful time.

For years, it had been his custom at the holiday season to send a personal Christmas card and New Year's greeting to hundreds of his closest friends and associates. There may no longer be anyone living who received one of those annual greetings, but they are highly treasured as family keepsakes by the relatives of persons now deceased who did receive them. The greeting usually had on it a photograph of Brother Van and a few words of cheer and inspiration. He had already prepared his greeting for the Christmas season of 1919. If he was still living, it would be sent out as it was. If he had died, John Martin was to send them out, after having the caption printed below Brother Van's picture, "First Christmas in Heaven."

The Reverend John Martin was in Brother Van's hospital room every minute he could spare from his essential duties. He was there when Miss Helen Piper and a group of children from the Deaconess School in Helena came to visit. Brother Van's young friends were no less concerned for him than the adults. They knew how much he loved Christmas, so they brought Christmas to him. Gathered around his bed, Miss Piper and the children visited with him a little, and then sang some Christmas carols. The aged minister lay there in his bed, tears of happiness streaming down his cheeks, and said to the Reverend Martin, "John, I tell you, that is the sweetest sound this side of heaven."

On Monday, December 15th, he had a second stroke, more severe than the first one. Paralysis began to spread to all parts of his body, rendering him almost completely helpless. Unable to eat, his strength ebbed rapidly. He was able to raise his right arm a little, but could move no other parts of his body. He gave up the fight to remain alive at this point and began to look forward to life eternal. He told Miss Ariss that when it was time for him to go to his heavenly home, he would raise his arm in a gesture of farewell to her and the others who may be present.

The *Great Falls Daily Tribune* on Wednesday, December 17th, 1919, carried the latest medical bulletin:

The Rev. Dr. W. W. Van Orsdel, known familiarly to all Montana as 'Brother Van,' is very near death at the Deaconess Hospital. Word from the hospital early this (Wed.) morning was to the effect that the end is expected hourly and it was regarded as improbable he could live until noon.

His condition has been growing worse since Monday, and Tuesday at noon it was thought he would not live out the day; but about the middle of the afternoon he showed slight improvement for a time. He again began to decline before last midnight and all hope of further substantial gain was abandoned.

On the following day, the same paper reported:

The condition of the Rev. W. W. Van Orsdel, pioneer minister whose death has been expected hourly for the past two days was reported at the Deaconess Hospital this morning as being unchanged, except that he has grown appreciably weaker during the day. The patient has been unable to take either medicine or nourishment since Tuesday and it is considered that any rally that may occur will be very brief in duration. Hope previously entertained for his recovery was abandoned the first of the week and news of his passing at any time will only mark that which has been known to his physician as inevitable for several days.

He was still able to speak some, and he had a few last words he wanted to say. He told John Martin to "tell the preachers not to lose heart." On a more general note, he said, "I haven't an enemy in the world—only friends. Tell the people of Montana that I love them all." Even in the act of dying, he was scattering seeds of love, hope and kindness on which the kingdom could be more firmly established.

Toward the evening on Thursday, Brother Van slipped into a state of unconsciousness. By midnight, his breathing had become more labored and shallow, and his already-feeble pulse grew weaker. The doctors, nurses and loved ones at his bedside knew the end had come. At 12:10 A. M. on Friday, December 19, he roused from his semi-coma just enough to be able to open his eyes and smile, and as he feebly lifted his right hand, he whispered his announcement of the heavenly vision, "Home! Home!"

His hand fell back upon the sheet, and everyone knew, without the physician's official pronouncement, that the beloved Brother Van was dead. His 1919 Christmas greeting would have the inscription "First Christmas in Heaven."

He hadn't been afraid to die, and his death had not been a grim experience for those who stood helplessly by, waiting for it to come. It had been a joyous homecoming, and they could not feel sad about his death. Those last two months of confinement had been a great agony for Brother Van. Bed was no place for W. W. Van Orsdel to be. What pained him much more than the illness was the stillness. He had places to go and people to see and sermons to preach and souls to save.

But, oh! what a sense of bereavement the people felt. They knew that in any given century of human history only a tiny handful of real giants are born, and for a certainty, Brother Van had been one of those. No memorial service could possibly express the sorrow that was upon the land. Every little village and hamlet, every city and farm home felt the enormity of the loss. He had been, truly, the best-loved man in Montana, and Montana has probably never before or since been in such a deep and universal state of mourning.

In recognition of his death, the state and national flags at the state capitol were lowered to half-staff—something which had never been done before, and hasn't been done since to honor any citizen not involved in government or the military.

The ninety-minute funeral service in the First Methodist Church in Great Falls on December 23 was both stately and personally touching, and drew a much larger number of mourners than the church could hold. Three of Brother Van's fellow ministers, plus a former Governor of Montana, delivered eulogies. Bishop Cooke was unable to be present, but wrote a statement about Brother Van that expressed what everyone felt. He said, in part:

> . . . I know men. I have met enough of them in every station of life to be able to sum up their dominant characteristics, and I knew Van Orsdel. Strong soul, like the mountains, rock-ribbed in moral strength—his very presence said, 'Here's a man!' And yet he was as kind and gentle and beautiful in his unconscious demeanor as a little child. Really big men always are. Brother Van was everybody's friend. I don't believe there was a dog in all Montana that would not wag its tail when he saw him coming. . . .Oh, friend of mine, how you loved!. . .If you would see his monument, look around.

A few hours after the church service, the Great Northern railway carried its famous passenger one last time from Great Falls to Helena. Burial services were held in the afternoon of December 24 at Forestvale Cemetery in the valley north of Helena, not far from the Deaconess School. In the gathering dusk of the Holy Night, a group of children and deaconesses trudged through the snow to the cemetery, bearing a small Christmas tree gaily decorated with things the children had made. Already frozen were the flowers that had been left there a few hours before, at the graveside service. Placing their little tree on the fresh mound of earth that covered the casket, the children lifted their tear-streaked faces to the sky and sang Christmas carols for the man whom they had loved as if he were their father, and who loved them as if he were their father. Of all the tributes given to honor him, Brother Van probably liked that one best of all.

When he turned 70 in 1918, Brother Van intended to retire. He had purchased 20 acres of land on the northwest shore of Flathead Lake—a place of surpassing beauty in northwest Montana. It was his intention to retire there with his brother Fletcher, build a cabin, and spend the remainder of his days resting and fishing. The presiding bishop and his fellow ministers implored him not to leave them, as they didn't see how they could survive without his great leadership and inspiring presence. He agreed to serve yet another year, and it proved to be his last year.

It is, of course, impossible to say whether he would have suffered the stroke and died that year, retired or not. Maintaining his usual administrative schedule was a severe strain, of course. But there is good reason to presume that his schedule would not have been much less busy had he retired. He had a way of getting involved, and he had done enough work in the Flathead area in earlier years to be very well-known there, as in the rest of the state. It doesn't seem likely he would have been left alone to enjoy a restful and peaceful retirement anywhere in Montana. It was typical of Brother Van to have given up his retirement dream in order to respond once more to the call of the church for his services.

Besides the Flathead Lake property, Brother Van had acquired three other pieces of property over the years. How, when, and why he obtained them is not recorded anywhere in his journals or letters, but he did own 600 acres near Sand Coulee (which is near Great Falls), 40 acres near Valier (about 75 miles north of Great Falls), and 200 acres near Waterloo (about 40 miles southeast of Butte). In his will, the Waterloo property was given to his brother Fletcher, and the other three parcels of land, valued at over $30,000, were given to the Deaconess School, Montana Wesleyan University, and the Great Falls Deaconess Hospital.

One thing we do know is that Brother Van acquired these properties in the early years when land was literally "dirt cheap" (pun intended). He had owned a few other parcels of land over the years, and had sold them to provide financing for some of his special projects such as the college, the children's school and the hospital. Or, the funds could have been used to pay his pledges for building churches and parsonages in various locations. One piece of property he bought for $320 and was able to sell some years later for $12,000. A parcel purchased for $500 was later sold for nearly $40,000. Such tremendous growth would be possible only if he had bought open land which proved later to be in the middle of a townsite. He was here early enough to have been able to do that, and smart enough to know what property he should purchase.

Gifts on record that Brother Van made to various efforts during his lifetime add up to over $30,000, which just might come near to equaling the total sum he was paid as salary in his 47 years of ministry. If to that is added the $30,000 he left in his will, it is a certainty that his gifts to the church exceeded 100% of all salaries paid him by the church. Brother Van obviously didn't believe in tithing; he would never think of giving so little as just a tenth of what he had.

He spent very little on the world's goods. He liked to have nice clothes, and he did, but his suits were usually bought for him by friends. When he ate on the train, he never went to the dining car for a full and costly meal, but bought a sandwich and a glass of milk to eat in his own car. With his clergy pass, he could ride the train free, and stagecoach drivers usually took their fare in song, and others, like the innkeeper at Horse Prairie, had him pay for his lodging with prayer. His way of life didn't demand the expenditure of a lot of cash. He was a very generous person, but he simply refused to spend anything that wasn't necessary for his own living, so that he would have more money available with which to do good for others.

Having no family or home, belonging to no group other than the church, and in all respects being completely unencumbered, Brother Van had absolutely no claims other than the church's upon his time, attention, concern and money.

The Reverend A. W. Hammer, a former cowboy whom Brother Van converted in the pioneer days, became a minister specializing in work with the Indians at Browning. In 1913 the ministers of the conference, honoring Brother Van with the gift of a fine gold watch, asked Brother Hammer to make the presentation in their behalf. In doing so, he told of how the early times had paved the way for the present times, and the significant role Brother Van played in that transition:

There was not a promising outlook for righteousness. But out of these bullwhackers, mule skinners, prospectors, gamblers and traders, with a vision that overlooked the highest peaks of the Rocky Mountains, they built and sang and prayed, and shouted themselves and the Kingdom to victory and took this land for Christ.

They have seen the watering place of the buffalo and the antelope become the camping place of the cowboy and the sheepherder, followed by the rancher and the farmer; the hamlet and the great city bound to the great country both east and west by ties of steel, along which rush the transcontinental trains. Or they have seen the wide spot in the road become the city that was now entertaining the conference.

To one of these I come to pay special tribute this afternoon. To the best-known and the most loved man in Montana, one whose name is lisped by little tots all over this great state, as they at mama's knee say their 'now I lay me down to sleep,' closing with 'God bless papa and mama, and God bless Brother Van.'. . .

At one end of the grave in Forestvale cemetery is a small stone bearing the inscription "Pioneer Minister—1848-1919." At the other end is a large rough-hewn boulder with only one space polished, just large enough to fit the name "BROTHER VAN."

An epitaph can't get much shorter than that. But just those two words, "BROTHER VAN," speak volumes to those who know his story.

PHOTO CREDITS

page vii   Montana Historical Society Photograph Archives

page 6   Yellowstone Conference (United Methodist) Historical Archives

page 65   Montana Historical Society Photograph Archives

page 81   Yellowstone Conference Historical Archives

page 125   Lena Boone, Dillon

page 171   Yellowstone Conference Historical Archives

page 184   Montana Historical Society Photograph Archives

page 196   Yellowstone Conference Historical Archives

page 209   Yellowstone Conference Historical Archives

page 221   Yellowstone Conference Historical Archives

page 224   Yellowstone Conference Historical Archives

page 233   Yellowstone Conference Historical Archives